Greenhill Books

WITH THE
FRENCH
FOREIGN
LEGION
IN SYRIA

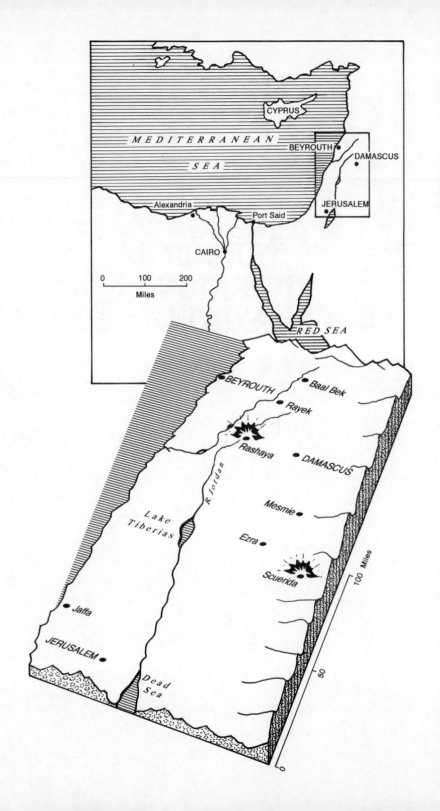

WITH THE
FRENCH
FOREIGN
LEGION
IN SYRIA

JOHN HARVEY

Greenhill Books, London
Stackpole Books, Pennsylvania

This edition of *With the French Foreign Legion in Syria*
first published 1995 by Greenhill Books
Lionel Leventhal Limited, Park House, 1 Russell Gardens
London NW11 9NN
and
Stackpole Books, 5067 Ritter Road, Mechanicsburg, PA 17055, USA

British Library Cataloguing in Publication Data
Harvey, John
With the French Foreign Legion in Syria.
—New ed
I. Title
956.9104092
ISBN 1–85367–212–2

Library of Congress Cataloging-in-Publication Data available

Publishing History
With the French Foreign Legion in Syria was first published as
With the Foreign Legion in Syria in 1928 (Hutchinson & Co., London),
and is now reproduced and enhanced with a new Introduction by
Martin Windrow and a new map by John Richards.

This book reflects the conventions and attitudes of the period in which it
was first published, and may contain language and sentiments that
would not be considered acceptable in a newly written work.

Printed and bound in Great Britain by
Biddles Ltd, Guildford and King's Lynn

CONTENTS

INTRODUCTION

As is not unusual among memoirists from the ranks of the
Legion before the Second World War, little reliable information is available about the author. Harvey is a pseudonym for a
man apparently named either Barrington or Hargreaves, who
was listed in U.S. Library of Congress records in 1937 as living
in Norfolk. He wrote several other books, as "Ex-Legionnaire
1384" or "Operator 1384"; and like several other adventurers
of the inter-war years—for instance, the better-documented
Adolph Cooper—he seems subsequently to have made something of a career retailing his real or supposed exploits.

One incident in this book—his desertion in company with
the American "Clare" and two Germans—is confirmed in the
better-known memoir *Legion of the Damned* by Bennett Doty
(1928); Doty served under the name Clare, and both he and
Harvey give similar names for their German fellow-deserters.
Apart from these meagre shreds of information, the reader
must judge *With the French Foreign Legion in Syria* upon its
own merits.

The book has two main claims on our interest: it is a perfect
archetype of a certain style of Legion memoir; and a rare voice
from the ranks of those few Legion units which fought the
1925–26 Druse uprising in Syria.

Since the appearance of the first known memoir by a non-
French ranker in the Legion (Lamping's brief account from
the 1830s), such books have fallen into two distinct cate-
gories. The first and most numerous, into which Harvey's

7

book falls, consists of the self-justifying deserter's tale: "My heroic escape from the living hell of the Foreign Legion...". The rarer type give more or less unflinching accounts of Legion life and campaigns, without any particular indignation or special pleading. Both usually give proper credit to the fighting qualities of the Legion, although the latter type— often by ex-soldiers with battle experience in other armies— frequently betray professional irritation at the limited resources or unimaginative doctrine which hampered the Legion's effectiveness in their day.

Whether or not the Welsh ex-coalminer Harvey's text was ghost-written for him by a journalist (and such purple phrases as "the broken playthings of Fate" might suggest that it was), it is ripe with the clichés of his time and nationality. Writing within a few years of the enormously popular publication of P.C. Wren's novel *Beau Geste*, which had obviously created a lively market for Legion tales, Harvey panders much more coarsely than even the tough-minded "gentleman ranker" Wren to Anglo-Saxon prejudices, and to a perceived public taste for gamey horrors. It is interesting to speculate what part the collective trauma of the Great War had played in shaping this taste.

The first two pages of Harvey's book set the tone: his fellow legionnaires are scum, degenerates, cut-throats—and, being foreigners, are "human refuse". He aims to thrill and titillate a far more easily shockable readership than today's with tales of bloody atrocity and casual vice. An informed response can only be, "well, up to a point...". There are obvious mistakes in minor matters of facts, for instance his misdating of the Syrian fighting by a year, and his identification of Sousse as the depot of the Foreign Legion rather than of the 1st Foreign Cavalry Regiment. While his general picture of French behaviour towards native populations, in an age long before the media enjoyed independent access to colonial campaigns, rings grimly true, some specific incidents are more obviously invented. The picture of his captain at Rachaya as a homicidal psychopath, and his repeated description of black troops being driven into battle with whips, are unconvincing to any reader familiar with the subject.

Nevertheless, one forms the impression that such *grand guignol* episodes are isolated inventions inserted to "spice up" a generally authentic picture. Harvey's book provides a useful contrast with the best-known Legion cavalry memoir of the interwar years, Weygand's admirable *Legionnaire*, which tells the story of the 1st Foreign Cavalry Regiment in Morocco some ten years after these events, and from the viewpoint of a junior officer. Taken as a whole the book is a valuable example of its genre, despite its sometimes frustrating lack of specifics such as dates and unit designations.

There seems no reason to doubt that Harvey did indeed fight as a trooper in Syria, which places him in the 4th Squadron of the 1st Foreign Cavalry Regiment (IV/1ere REC). The action fought in defence of "Mesmie" cannot be identified with any confidence; it does not square in any detail with descriptions of the major battle at Mousseifre, 17 September 1925, fought by IV/1ere REC and the infantry of V/4e REI under Commandant Kratzert (of which Bennett Doty gives an impressive account). Nevertheless, Harvey's description of the general character of the campaign viewed from the French ranks is interesting.

We are on surer ground with the battle of Rachaya, 20–24 November 1925. The units which held this ruined mediaeval fort, awkwardly placed for defence in the middle of a Syrian village, were Harvey's IV/1ere REC under Captain Landriau, and an Arab regular cavalry squadron of the 12th (Tunisian) Spahis under Captain Granger, who commanded the garrison until his death on the 22nd. This isolated position was first attacked by a strong force of Druses during evening watering call on the 20th.

Initially repulsed, the Druses maintained their attacks for three days and nights. The village buildings covered them close up to the French perimeter, and at one point they captured part of the fort, killing the cavalry horses and engaging the garrison in prolonged hand-to-hand fighting. Small angles and positions changed hands back and forth in desperate bayonet and grenade charges. By the morning of the 24th, when French aircraft attacked the Druses and a relief force from the 6th Spahis arrived, the survivors were down to less than a dozen cartridges per man. The 4th Squadron, 1st Foreign Cavalry had lost 58 dead and wounded (Harvey's mention of 35 fit survivors puts this figure in context); and the unit was subsequently cited in Army orders, and awarded the lanyard in the colours of the *Croix de Guerre TOE* (War Cross for Exterior Theatres of Operations).

Harvey's account of his desertion is typical of the period, though he was unusually lucky to serve only 18 months of his eight-year sentence. Historically, the Legion's treatment of deserters varied from summary punishment but robust toleration of brief, drunken excursions, to the harshest penalties for those who made determined attempts, particularly in time of war and carrying their weapons.

The vast expansion of the Legion in the 1920s certainly led to a relaxation in the standards previously demanded of, and enforced by, not only the all-important long service NCOs, but also elements of the officer corps. Complaints about the relative lack of reliability of some units even on active service, and about a continuing high level of desertion, are to be found in many internal memoranda passed between veteran senior officers during the 1920s and early 1930s.

Harvey's book is important in this context. It was the recognition by the authorities of the vital need to counter the poor discipline and morale which dogged some units in Harvey's day which led directly to the conscious policy of creating a positive ethos specific to the corps. This process of shaping—even inventing—a body of tradition which would set the Legion apart and give it back its pride was carried out from the early 1930s, with lasting success, by the legendary Paul Rollet, "Father of the Legion".

Martin Windrow, 1995

With the
Foreign Legion in Syria

CHAPTER I

JOINING THE LEGION

THERE are two Foreign Legions ,of France.
One exists only in the imagination of
romantic novelists and is chiefly composed
of strong, silent heroes destined to fall in love
with charming ladies in due course. The other,
which happens to be real, has its headquarters at
Sousse, in Northern Africa, and is composed of
human scum.

The average legionnaire is frankly a blackguard; generally he is a fugitive from justice.
The recruiting officials ask no questions, and any
man who can hold a rifle, shoot, and be shot, is
good enough for them. The result is that Sousse
can boast a selection of murderers, thieves,
crooks, thugs, and degenerates, which makes the
Dartmoor collection appear quite mild in comparison. The Legion, in short, is the cut-throat's

sure asylum. He has only to promise to serve France with honour and fidelity for five years and he is safe from his pursuers.

The real Legion is a very useful institution. It segregates some thousands of undesirables in the African desert, and most of them die there. It is civilization's dustbin, and it is always ready to receive more human refuse for the incinerator.

It should certainly be avoided by all really nice heroines.

To understand the Legion it is necessary to remember that central fact—that it is composed chiefly of moral derelicts. The human brute is the lowest of all animals, and he cannot be controlled by kid-glove methods. The lash is the only argument he understands. He cannot sink lower in the scheme of things ; it is impossible for him to rise higher. He is one of the damned.

But he can, and does, drag others down to his own bestial level.

That is the horror and the tragedy of Legion— the brutalizing degradation. Officers, N.C.O.s and men, they are all in the grip of the brute. Nobody yet came into contact with the Legion without being worse for the experience. Even the beggars draw their rags aside and spit their hatred and contempt at the legionnaires as they pass.

Scum !

It was not because I was a fugitive from justice that I joined the Legion. I was hungry.

I was born in a South Wales mining village, and at fourteen I was earning my living underground. At seventeen I was in Flanders with the South Wales Borderers, being afterwards wounded in the head at Ypres. The War over, I went back to the mine.

Then came the slump, and I was one of the thousands who were thrown out of work. But I was of too restless and adventurous a nature to take kindly to inactivity, and at last I set off to seek my fortune.

Early in 1925 I found myself in London, and that fortune seemed as far off as ever. I was down and out, desperate, and ready for the first adventure that presented itself. I would go anywhere and do anything. I wanted only to escape from that weary, hungry existence.

Such was the position when, one cheerless afternoon in February, I entered a Church Army hostel in Marylebone. There was the usual collection of hard-luck cases, but there was one man who struck me as being of a better class than the others. His name, he told me, was Alfred Whittingham, and he was an old soldier who had seen service in India, France, and other parts of the world. Like the rest of us, he was down and out, waiting for the first adventure that offered itself.

While we were sitting near the fire, swapping Army experiences and yarning about things in general, another man came over to us and stood listening to our talk.

"You two fellows seem keen on soldiering," he remarked after a time.

"More or less," we admitted.

"Then why don't you join the French Foreign Legion ?" he asked. "A pal of mine joined some time ago and he's doing fine. In addition to his pay of ten francs a day they gave him a bonus of 5,000 francs. He tells me, too, that he's expecting to get a stripe soon."

Whittingham and I glanced at each other. Ten francs a day and a bonus of 5,000 francs sounded good to a couple of penniless out-of-works. This was the sort of thing we had been looking for.

"I only wish I were ten years younger," continued our new friend. "You wouldn't find me here wasting my time !"

"How do you join the Legion ?" I asked.

"It's easy enough," he answered. "All you have to do is to go along to the French Consulate in Bedford Square. They'll put you wise."

It was not long before Whittingham and I decided that we would have to look into this. Our unknown friend might have been guilty of a little exaggeration, but we could surely rely upon any information we might get from the Consulate.

"We've come to inquire about the Foreign Legion," we explained on our arrival at Bedford Square.

We could not have been received more politely.

"Ah, you wish to join the famous Legion?" asked the official who was attending to us.

"We're thinking about it. Is it true that the pay's ten francs a, day and that there's a bonus of 5,000 francs as well?"

We were assured that it was perfectly true. Moreover, the food was of the choicest and the prospects dazzling. Indeed, for men of adventure the Legion was the ideal life. A couple of smart young men with some experience of soldiering already would inevitably find themselves sergeants before long. And it would be merely in the ordinary nature of things if in due course they were sent to the Military College at St. Cyr and given their commissions.

"And after a year's service," we were told, "the legionnaire is entitled to a month's leave in Paris on full pay."

Whittingham looked at me and I looked at Whittingham. Why hadn't we heard of the Foreign Legion before?

"You think you wish to join?" we were asked.

"We most certainly do!"

"*Bon!* Then first of all we will see if you succeed in passing the medical examination!"

We were sent to see a French doctor and I was very anxious lest I should fail to pass the medical examination. I am of the lean and wiry kind, and nobody has ever described me as a typical guardsman. Moreover, hunger and worry had not improved my physique.

But my anxiety was unfounded. The doctor was a genial soul with an enthusiasm for the Legion, and he was much too busy telling us yarns to bother about our physical condition. He did not even ask us to cough or to say "ninety-nine".

Needless to say, we passed the "medical examination" with flying colours, and at the Consulate we were gravely informed that we were among the lucky ones who are able to join the Legion and win fame and fortune.

I am afraid Whittingham and I must have shocked some of the sober inhabitants of Bedford Square. At last, after months of hunger and despair, our luck had changed. Soon we would be drawing our ten francs a day and would feel that bonus bulging in our pockets! We laughed till we cried. We slapped one another on the back. We called each other *"Mon Capitaine"*, and started an argument as to whether we should open our month's leave in Paris with a visit to the Moulin Rouge or the Foliès Bergère.

If we had had any money we should probably have been drunk within an hour. But we hadn't.

The next formality was obtaining our passports. We were warned that the British authorities, for some unknown reason, refused to issue passports to men proceeding to join the Legion, so in our applications we stated that we wanted to visit the War graves.

My passport was the first to be issued and, on presenting myself at the Consulate, I was given a bulky envelope, which presumably contained my papers, and packed straight off to Dover. Whittingham, I was told, would follow in the course of a day. This was rather a pity, for we had already arranged to be pals and would have preferred to travel together. My orders were

definite, however, and we had to content ourselves with arranging to meet at the earliest
opportunity somewhere in France.

A few hours later I felt once again the throb
of a cross-Channel steamer and watched the
white cliffs of England receding into the distance.
I was a soldier once more, wondering what the
future held for me and whether I should ever see
those cliffs again. I remembered the forlorn little
mining village which was my home, with its
dreary coal tips and drab slag heaps. I pictured
myself returning in two or three years' time in
the smart blue uniform of an officer of the
French Army.

Why not ? I asked myself. At the Consulate
they had told me that there was no reason why
I should not win my way to St. Cyr and a commission. Why not ?

My luck had changed at last, and I was determined to make the most of it ! It was still good
to be alive !

CHAPTER II

I WAS still dreaming of heroic adventure and that bonus of 5,000 francs when we reached Calais. I was also aware of the fact that I had a first-class appetite. Food had not been over plentiful of late, and though the French authorities had given me my ticket and paid all the other expenses, they had not been very generous in the way of pocket money. A few francs on account and a square meal would have been very acceptable.

As I stepped off the gangway I was greeted by the French Army agent who had, apparently, been sent to meet me. He was a smartly-dressed young civilian with a most impressive beard. He accepted the envelope containing my papers, and together we set off for the barracks. He spoke excellent English, but he was neither so affable nor so communicative as his compatriots in Bedford Square, and he did not regale me with cheery anecdotes about the Legion.

I did not worry, however, at his omission to congratulate me on my good fortune. I was too busy wondering whether the cook-house at the barracks was in a position to cope with my needs.

My luck was in again. We arrived at the barracks most opportunely, and within half an hour I was being directed to the mess-room.

That mess-room was my first shock. Dozens of men were crowded at long tables, all of them jabbering and yelling at the top of their voices. The tables were thick with grease and the relics of past meals; the floor was filthy and littered with scraps of food. Lumps of unappetizing-looking bread were being passed down the tables from hand to hand.

One glance at the scene would have given a British sergeant-major an apoplectic fit.

But I was too hungry to worry. And my War experiences had left me with no great opinion of either the manners or the cleanliness of the French. I took a seat at one of the tables and joined in the scramble, successfully snatching one of the largest pieces of bread.

Dixies were brought in and placed one on each table. Taking a pile of plates, the lance-corporal in charge dished out a cupful of alleged soup to each plate which was then passed down from hand to hand. Naturally, a good deal was spilled in the process, with the result that the people at the bottom of the table became more demonstrative and noisier than ever. Their more fortunately-placed comrades sopped up the soup that had been spilled with their bread.

The rest of the meal consisted of horse-flesh and a small ration of musty haricot beans. As with the soup, these were served out by the lance-corporal and passed from hand to hand down the table. If a man liked the look of a certain portion he kept it for himself; if he didn't, he passed it on. Again the unfortunates at the lower end of the table expressed their sense of injustice by shouting and gesticulating wildly.

On the whole it was not a very encouraging start to what was intended to be a brilliant military career, and I could not help comparing that pigsty meal with the spick-and-span orderliness of the British Army. I comforted myself with the thought that things would doubtless be better when I became a fully fledged legionnaire. And I was not forgetting the good pay and the bonus; for their sake I was prepared to put up with a good deal.

The following morning I was paraded before the Commandant, who told me that I would proceed at once to Dunkirk where, I gathered, was the chief recruiting station for the Legion.

Immediately on my arrival at the barracks at Dunkirk I was paraded before a recruiting officer and a doctor. What struck me as an unusual feature for a medical examination was the fact that a girl was busy typing in the same room.

"You are fit?" asked the doctor in excellent English.

"Yes, sir."

"You saw a doctor in London?"

"Yes, sir," I answered, remembering the so-called medical examination in London.

"You'll do. Sign your papers."

I wonder what proportion of the recruits for the Foreign Legion are rejected on medical grounds!

The doctor having satisfied himself that I was as sound as a bell, the typist stepped forward and did her little bit. Taking an official-looking document, she gabbled it off at a tremendous speed. I listened respectfully, but naturally did not understand a word.

"You understand?" asked the officer in charge.

"No, sir."

"It doesn't matter," he said. "It's your contract by which you agree to serve France with honour and fidelity for five years. Sign here."

I duly signed.

I would have liked to ask whether the contract contained any reference to the pay of ten francs a day, the bonus of 5,000 francs, and the month's leave in Paris after a year's service. It occurred to me that these important matters, which had played so prominent a part in the London conversations, had receded very much into the background since my arrival in France. But I could only hope for the best. Having proceeded so far it was too late to turn back—and in any case I had nothing to which to return.

It will be observed that I was not required to take any oath of allegiance to France or in any way to renounce my nationality. It was a purely business contract—though rather one-sided.

At Dunkirk I was not greatly impressed with my fellow recruits for the Legion. They were mostly Germans and Russians, and all were down and out. Few had washed and several were in rags. Being still something of an optimist, I assured myself that with such a rabble it would not be long before I was promoted to non-commissioned rank.

There was nothing in particular to do at the barracks and, feeling somewhat lonely as the solitary representative of Britain in this collection of human refuse, I applied for an evening pass. Rather to my surprise it was granted.

Money was still scarce, and the English Sailors' Home was the nearest approach to a gay evening within my reach. But it was a treat to hear English voices again, and it was not long before I was chatting with some sailors round the fire.

"You poor fool!" exclaimed one of them when I mentioned that I had joined the Legion. "You don't know what you've let yourself in for! Half the scum o' Europe's in the Legion! It's like a convict settlement—only worse! 'Struth, I'd sooner commit suicide than join that mob!"

"Anyhow," I answered, rather nettled at his tone, "the pay's good and there's a fine bonus in addition. What's more, there's a first-class chance of getting a commission later on."

My blunt friend replied with a bellow of laughter.

"I don't think!" he said. "All those yarns about the good pay and the wonderful bonus are just the bait to catch mugs like yourself! As for getting a commission, you don't stand an earthly —unless you're rolling in money! The fact is,

24

my boy, you've been sold a pup, and if you take my advice you'll slip quietly on board a British cargo boat and clear out while you've got the chance! I'll help smuggle you aboard, if you like."

"Thanks," I answered, "but I'm going through with it."

"Just as you like," he said with a shrug of his shoulders. "You'll be sorry later on. Within six months, if the jackals aren't already gnawing at your bones in the desert, you'll be trying your damnedest to desert."

I was in a meditative mood when I returned to the barracks. I realized that it was at any rate possible that my plain-spoken friend at the Sailors' Home had hit upon the truth. Perhaps I was no more than a credulous "mug". Perhaps I was a fool not to accept his offer to help me smuggle myself on board a British vessel and make my way back to England.

But it needed more than a stranger's words to tempt me to return to the weary, hungry existence I had left. Civilization had given me nothing and I was willing to give barbarism a trial. Besides, there was a chance my critic was wrong. Perhaps, in spite of his sneering remarks, I was destined to become an officer of the Legion.

In any case, I was going through with it. I had promised to serve France faithfully for five years, and I was ready to carry out my part of the bargain—provided I received a square deal.

The following day, in the company of about fifty other recruits for the Legion—a nondescript crowd of Russians, Germans, Bulgarians, Danes, Serbs, Poles, and Swiss—I was sent to Marseilles. On our arrival we were marched to Fort St. Jean, and it was here that I received my first pay.

It worked out at exactly half a franc a day !

CHAPTER III

OUR stay at the old grim fortress of St. Jean at Marseilles was comparatively pleasant. We were still *en route* for the Legion, and our careers would not begin in earnest until we reached the depot at Sousse. Meanwhile, our chief occupation was performing various fatigues. We enjoyed, on the whole, what is known in military circles as a "cushy time". The food was better than at Calais and Dunkirk, and there was at least a show of cleanliness and orderliness.

I don't know whether the economy cry is popular in France, but if so the taxpayers may be pleased to learn that there was no undue hurry in issuing us with our uniforms. We were still wearing our civilian clothes, or what was left of them, and the result was that when we paraded we looked as choice a collection of tramps as ever lined up in the casual ward. One morning I amazed my foreign comrades, especially the Russians, by washing my one and only shirt and—it would inevitably have been stolen if I had hung it up to dry—putting it on again whilst it was still wet. It was not very comfortable, but at any rate it was clean, and by the grace of God I did not develop pneumonia. The others, however, regarded the incident as another remarkable instance of the hopeless eccentricity of the English.

A day or two after my arrival another batch of recruits turned up, and amongst them was Alfred Whittingham, the pal who had joined up with me in London. Naturally, I was more than glad to see him again, and it was not long before we were having a heart-to-heart talk. We agreed that, so far as we could see, we had been badly swindled. Not one of the dazzling promises held out to us in London had been, or appeared likely to be, fulfilled.

Of course, we had no means of obtaining redress. If we had protested nobody would have paid any attention—except perhaps to put us on the harder and more unpleasant fatigues. We had been caught in the trap, and the only course open to us was to hope for the best and go through with it. But we both agreed that those contracts

28

by which we had undertaken to serve France with fidelity and honour for five years were scraps of paper obtained by false pretences.

There was one man among the recruits at Marseilles who stood out from the others. Even in his worn and shabby clothes he was obviously an aristocrat. There was breeding in his every movement, and he had the saddest-looking eyes I have ever seen.

In addition to his native Russian, he could speak English, French, and German perfectly, and it was not long before a friendship sprang up between us. In the old days he had been a prince, owning an immense estate in Georgia, where he had lived in feudal state in a centuries-old castle. He had also been a captain in the Imperial Army and private courier to the Czar.

The Revolution had brought him to ruin. The Bolshevists had burned his castle and murdered his wife and children. After innumerable hair's-breadth escapes, he had succeeded in getting across the frontier. Penniless, he had tried to earn his living in several ways. Finally, he had joined the Legion in the hope of ultimately obtaining a commission.

His hopes, by the way, were doomed to disappointment. Long afterwards I heard that he had been sentenced to eight years' imprisonment for attempting to desert from the Legion.

Naturally, his experiences had left their mark on him. Sometimes he was bitter and morose; at others he would be recklessly gay; occasionally he sought forgetfulness in a wild drinking bout. But behind it all there was one of the most charming personalities I have ever met. I have often watched him and pictured him as he used to be in the old days—with his wife and kiddies in his great castle, or in St. Petersburg, resplendent in the uniform of a captain of the Imperial Guard.

"Well," I said to him one day, "I've often thought that Fate must have a grudge against me, but compared with you I've been revelling in her smiles!"

"I'm one of the lucky ones!" he answered with his devil-may-care laugh. "There are hundreds of my friends and relations who have suffered infinitely more than I!"

He went on to describe in the calm, simple way of a man who is telling of things that he has actually seen, the fate of some of his friends of the old days. It was like listening to a man who has escaped from a world of hideous, nauseating horror. Even now, with my life in the Legion behind me, I shudder at the memory of what he told me of the incredible tortures suffered by his fellow aristocrats at the hands of those obscene, blood-maddened mobs.

"I have always one thing to be thankful for," he said. "My wife and daughter were merely murdered."

And he meant it, in all sincerity.

Some may consider him nothing more than a loose-living drunkard. But I am proud to have been his friend.

Russians formed the majority of the recruits for the Legion, most of them being refugees from the Bolshevists. Germans were the next most numerous, practically everyone of them being a criminal. Of the two, I preferred the Russians ; they were comparatively honest.

After we had spent a few days at Fort St. Jean in scrubbing floors, carrying stores, and grousing, we were all paraded, and volunteers for the Cavalry were called for.

I was not an expert horseman, but I was tempted. I remembered how, when serving with the Infantry in the War, I had often envied the lot of the Cavalry. And Whittingham, who was standing beside me, was obviously hesitating also.

"What about it ?" I whispered.

"Let's !" he whispered back.

We both stepped forward. And at the same time Georgia, as we called the prince, volunteered as well.

We were promptly marched off and put through a riding test under the supervision of a troop sergeant. The test, like most of the examinations connected with the Legion, was a farce. We had merely to trot round a ring two or three times, and those who succeeded in keeping their seats were duly accepted for the Cavalry.

That afternoon it occurred to Georgia that it would be a good idea to ask for permission to spend a few hours in the town. Hitherto, all we had seen of Marseilles was the interior of Fort St. Jean. Whittingham, having been detailed for a fatigue, was unfortunately unable to participate in the scheme, but a carefully-selected party of four, consisting of Georgia, another Russian, a Dane, and myself, succeeded in obtaining an interview with the Captain. Georgia acted as our spokesman, and explained how anxious we were to see the famous seaport of which we had heard so much.

"Hmph !" said the Captain, smoothing his beard, "I'll give you a pass each, up to eleven

32

o'clock to-night. See that you behave your-
selves."

Elated at our success, we lost no time in going
down to the town. Naturally the first—and as it
turned out the only—place of interest which we
visited was a café, where we celebrated our
holiday with a bottle of *vin rouge.*

The wine loosened our tongues, and it was not
long before the Dane was telling us the story of
why he had joined the Legion.

The boy—he was little more than that—was the
son of a shipping merchant in a fairly prosperous
way of business, and on leaving school had
entered his father's office. The father, I gathered,
was of the grim tyrannical type, and expected
his son to do the work of two men in return for
a meagre allowance. All had gone well, however,
until the boy met and fell in love with a girl some
years older than himself.

The lady, seemingly, was extravagant in her
tastes and exacting in her demands. The boy's
modest allowance was hopelessly inadequate.
Unable to break the spell of the charmer's
fascination, the lad took to gambling and to
embezzling his father's money. The girl, learning
what was happening, became more and more
insistent in her demands. The boy, in his desperate

efforts to extricate himself, sank deeper and deeper into the mire. At last the inevitable day of reckoning came. He found himself face to face with the fact that within a few hours his father would learn the truth.

In a frenzy of despair he dashed round to the girl's flat and begged her to run away with him. But she only laughed at him and told him that she had no use for a fool with no money. She was finished with him.

"I was mad," said the Dane simply, as he fingered his wineglass. "I did not know what I was doing. I only knew that my fingers were at her throat, that I was strangling the life out of her. I remember, too, how I laughed at her vain struggles."

At length he had flung her, senseless, to the floor and dashed blindly away. He had never learnt whether he had actually murdered the girl or not, but somehow he had managed to escape across the frontier.

"So I joined the Legion," he concluded. "There was nothing else to do."

There are many such as he sweating out their lives in the Legion of the Damned—the broken playthings of Fate.

It was over the second bottle of *vin rouge*

34

that Koryalov, the Russian, told us his story.

He had served with the Russian Army during the War, and afterwards with General Wrangel's Army. On the final break-up of that ill-fated enterprise, he found himself a fugitive whose one hope lay in his being able to reach the frontier and smuggle himself across to safety. In the course of his wanderings he had found another fugitive—a girl of aristocratic birth who had suffered unspeakable tortures from the Bolshevists, but had succeeded in escaping. Together they had pushed westwards, tramping by night, sleeping by day in the woods or any other shelter, and living on such food as they could steal and on roots. For weeks this existence continued ; then exposure and her past experiences took their inevitable toll and the girl fell ill. Hidden in a forest, Koryalov did his best to nurse her back to health, but it was a hopeless task. One morning at dawn the girl died in his arms.

He scraped a shallow grave with his hands and buried her as best he could. Then, having muttered the first prayer that had come to his lips for years, he continued on his way.

For a long time after Koryalov had told his story Georgia remained silent, a bitter look in his eyes. I could guess that he was thinking of his own experiences, of his murdered wife and children. Then suddenly his mood changed to one of reckless gaiety.

"Come on, boys !" he cried. "Let's drown our sorrows !"

He called for more *vin rouge*, and thereafter there was a constant succession of bottles. We grew more and more noisy. Georgia jumped on to a barrel and sang the songs of his native land. Then I was pushed forward amidst demands for "Tipperary"—several of them were convinced that it was the British National Anthem. Finally, we were all kicked out of the café. Then, arm-in-arm and singing at the tops of our voices, we staggered back towards Fort St. Jean, where the sergeant of the guard promptly bundled the lot of us into the cells.

The following morning I awoke with a severe headache and an uneasy suspicion that there was trouble ahead. I could see Georgia and the rest of us performing all the most unpleasant fatigues for many a day.

However, it was no use to grumble. We had had our little hour of freedom—and *vin rouge*—and must pay for it.

But a surprise awaited us. After the sergeant

had called us all the names in his extensive repertoire, we were paraded before the Commandant—who announced that, with the other volunteers for the Cavalry, we were to embark for Tunis at noon. Not a word about our escapade of the previous evening !

Perhaps the Commandant had forgotten it. Perhaps he had a sense of humour and knew what was awaiting us on the other side of the Mediterranean.

It was a broiling hot afternoon when we landed at Tunis and were marched through the dirty but picturesque town to the barracks.

Conditions had been fairly good at Marseilles. There had been an attempt at cleanliness, and the food had been more or less respectable. But at Tunis the barracks were filthy, the blankets verminous, and the food rotten. The heat only served to emphasize the general beastliness.

The discipline, too, was much harsher. The day after our arrival we were set on building a wall. From morn till night we toiled in our ragged civilian clothes under the blistering sun. Several collapsed under the strain. Some of the Germans talked of mutiny, but it came to nothing. We just sweated on, like convicts.

At last, to our infinite relief, we were marched to the railway station, herded into cattle-trucks—two dozen to a truck and a temperature of about 100 in the shade !—and transported to Sousse, the depot of the Legion.

CHAPTER IV

SOUSSE

SOUSSE, the depot of the Legion, is a rather jolly little seaport with a charming view of the Mediterranean. The great majority of the inhabitants are Italians and the next most numerous are the Arabs. There are comparatively few French and the usual cosmopolitan odds and ends to be found in every North African seaport.

The Commandant at the depot was a German, and he had a most refreshing passion for cleanliness. After the dirt and squalor of the barracks at Tunis and the Fort St. Jean at Marseilles, it was a glorious treat to see some freshly-scrubbed tables and floors again. Even the blankets were clean, which is saying a lot in a hot climate. Indeed, it was not uncommon for a man to be sentenced to the cells for a dirty uniform.

We recruits, however, were still wearing the "civvies" in which we had joined up—or what was left of them. I was better off than most, for I had a needle and some cotton and so was able to mend the worst of the rents in my clothes. But that needle and cotton unfortunately were useless when it was a question of mending boots, and one sole and upper celebrated our arrival at Sousse by definitely parting company with each other. I achieved a certain amount of comparative comfort by tying a piece of string round my foot.

On the second day after our arrival the long-deferred event took place, and we were ordered to parade on the barrack square before the quartermaster's stores. After we had stood for about a quarter of an hour in the broiling sun the Commandant arrived with one of the grubbiest and most loquacious old Jews I have ever seen. The Jew was carrying several empty sacks.

"Strip !" ordered the Commandant.

Every stitch of clothing we possessed had to be taken off, and there we stood—two long ranks of stark naked men, each with a little heap of clothing at his feet. Never had I known the sun's rays be fiercer than they were that afternoon ; and never had I known the flies be more persistent in their attentions. It seemed as if all the flies in Africa had assembled on that barrack square for the occasion. Most of the troops in the depot, too, were lounging about the square and making rude remarks about us.

Each man in turn had to take his bundle of rags to the spot where the Commandant and the Jew dealer were standing. The latter, who did not cease talking for an instant, pawed at the clothes and proclaimed eloquently that they were not worth a *sou*. The Commandant, paying no attention to his remarks, glanced at the clothes and barked out the price which he placed upon them—five francs, ten francs, or whatever other figure occurred to him. The Jew, declaring that he was ruined, bundled the clothes into his sack and counted out the money. The naked legionnaire then marched off to the quartermaster's stores, another took his place, and the whole performance began again, the Jew keeping up a constant flow of protest and lamentation and the Commandant ignoring his eloquence completely.

I was one of the lucky ones and received fifteen francs for my rags—a small fortune !

In the quartermaster's stores we received our kit, uniforms, underclothing, boots, and other necessaries. Quartermasters and their assistants are much the same the whole world over, and they all have weird and wonderful ideas as to what constitutes a good fit. And those at Sousse were no exception to the rule. The unfortunate recruit who protested that a cap which came over his ears was too large, or that a shirt which failed to meet round his neck was too small, was dismissed as a hopeless eccentric and warned that, if he was not careful, his habit of grumbling for grumbling's sake would get him into serious trouble.

Later on, however, we were able to make some adjustments in the barracks. The man whose boots were too large had no difficulty in finding a man whose boots were too small, and so, by a process of wholesale exchange, we ultimately arrived at a state of comparative comfort. Being on the small side, I was fortunate, for it was much easier to put a reef in a garment which was too big than to expand one which was too small.

And in any case, after looking and feeling like a tramp for so long, it was good to get into a decent uniform again and clean underclothing.

We were now full-blown legionnaires and our time was no longer wholly occupied in scavenging, sweeping, scrubbing, and similar fatigues. We were told off to squadrons, and our training began in earnest.

The following was the programme for an average day :

6 a.m.—Reveille, celebrated with a cup of coffee and a slice of black bread (no butter, margarine, or jam !).

6.30-9.30.—Riding exercise.

9.30-10.—Groom horses and clean harness.

10-11.—Sabre and rifle drill.

11.—Dinner, followed by a siesta during which our chief occupation was cursing the swarms of flies.

1-2.—Arms drill.

2-3.—Groom and water horses.

3-4.—Riding exercise.

4.—Groom horses and dismiss.

In addition, of course, there were the usual fatigues which form part of every soldier's life.

It was a strenuous existence, and it required a tough constitution to stand up to it. The riding-masters were as hard-bitten a crowd as ever I have met. Most of them were Cossacks, wonderful horsemen but devils to serve under.

The man who could not ride well had a very thin time. He was cursed and damned, and called every variety of pig and dog. A slash with a whip was quite a common occurrence—and those Cossacks were experts in the use of a long-thonged short-handled whip. Generally, the back was the spot

43

they selected, and I have seen an unfortunate comrade with half a dozen weals between his shoulder-blades. On one occasion an officer slashed a sergeant across the face, and he bore the mark for days. After that, ordinary troopers like myself regarded an occasional stinging cut between the shoulders as a normal dispensation of providence. And we certainly developed into first-class horsemen.

Life at Sousse, however, was not all hard work and no play. We had sports—horse-racing, swimming and boxing. And sometimes some energetic soul would get up a concert. These were very cosmopolitan affairs, songs being sung in every European language, with and without accompaniment. The audience, although unable to understand the words of most of the songs, applauded with impartial enthusiasm. One very popular turn was a really clever conjuror, who in the past had had a distinguished career as a swindler. And there was a wonderful pianist who was reputed to have committed several murders.

At these concerts I was often called upon to sing "Tipperary". The average foreigner apparently believes that this is the British National Anthem and is sung by every Englishman on every possible occasion. This was certainly the belief of most of the men in the Legion, and my efforts to disillusion them were always received with incredulous smiles.

Another great institution was pay-day, which came once a fortnight. The past and future being matters which the average legionnaire was anxious only to forget, practically the whole pay was promptly squandered in *vin rouge*, with the result that by nightfall most of us were blissfully drunk. The authorities very wisely turned a blind eye to these carousals, and it was only when tempers were lost and a free fight developed, which was fairly often, that disciplinary action was taken. Those who got drunk without quarrelling were left in peace until reveille the next morning when, if we were lucky, the coffee was extra-strong.

On these pay-day debauches the various nationalities used to forgather and each get drunk in its own particular fashion. The Russians were the quietest and the quickest. They just swilled themselves into unconsciousness, becoming more and more morose all the time. The Germans, on the other hand, indulged in community singing, roaring student songs at the tops of their voices. The singing was very good—or perhaps we weren't very critical—and often the officers used to come and listen, doing their bit towards the entertainment by filling up the wine jugs.

In the Legion a man does not drink for convivial reasons. He drinks with the fixed determination of becoming drunk as soon as possible. Superior folk will doubtless be horrified at such a degraded idea—but degradation is the keynote of the Legion. There the past is a thing of bitter regret and wasted opportunity ; and the future contains nothing more inviting than the prospect of a nameless grave in the African desert. In the Legion of the Damned they only really live when they are drunk. It is only then that they succeed in recapturing, just for a little while, those lost and shattered dreams.

"It's worth it, Harvey," my friend "Georgia" said to me one day when he was recovering from a particularly heavy bout. "It gives me the only thing I ask of life—forgetfulness."

If ever *vin rouge* was a blessing it is to those poor devils whom Fate has herded into the Legion.

Whittingham and I were very excited when our first pay-day came. We were told that we were not only to receive our pay, but also half of that famous bonus. It was the first time it had been mentioned since we had crossed the Channel.

We had long since had a suspicion that the pay was not ten francs a day, as we had been promised in London, but we still had lingering hopes of the 5,000 francs bonus.

Those hopes were soon blasted. Our pay proved to be at the rate of half a franc a day, and we received 250 francs as half of the bonus. The other 250 francs, we were told, would be paid at the end of three months.

We decided to complain to the Commandant. "In London we were promised ten francs a day and a bonus of 5,000 francs," we told him.

"I never heard such nonsense!" declared the Commandant. "Whoever told you that story made a very big mistake. The bonus is 250 francs now and a further 250 francs in three months' time. It is laid down in the Regulations. Let me hear no more of this foolish talk! Dismiss!"

We dismissed.

Some of us were so disgusted with the way in which we had been swindled that we discussed the possibility of deserting. We decided, however, that the risks were too great, at any rate while we were still at Sousse.

Some time before six Russians had made the attempt and the result had not been encouraging. Taking a couple of rifles and some ammunition, they had slipped down to the quay, stolen a motor-boat, and made off in the hope of reaching Malta.

By the time they were missed they had gained a start of nearly half an hour. But unfortunately they had been seen and troops were sent off in pursuit in a powerful motor-launch. The small boat with its desperate crew was soon sighted and a shot was fired by way of warning. The fire was returned with interest, and soon a running fight developed with the powerful launch continually gaining on the smaller vessel. Then the escaping Russians found that their supply of petrol had given out.

Surrender meant imprisonment and they decided to fight to a finish. They did, and all that the launch brought back to Sousse was a bullet-spattered and blood-stained motor-boat.

During the time that I was at Sousse there was only one man who succeeded in deserting from the Legion, and he had the advantage of outside help. Houssmann was a German, and, being a fine, upstanding lad, he caught the eye of Louise, the pretty little Belgian girl who was employed in one of the cafés in the town. Their friendship soon ripened into love and, there being no facilities for marriage in the Legion, they came to the

48

conclusion that the only thing to be done was to run off together.

Louise undertook all the arrangements. She went down to the harbour and succeeded in coaxing the captain of a trading steamer into agreeing to stow her and her lover away in the hold in return for a sum of 600 francs. She then acquired a complete set of "civvies" for Houssmann.

The steamer was due to sail in the evening, and that day Houssmann applied for an all-night pass which, in view of his exemplary conduct, was granted.

The following morning the steamer had sailed, Houssmann was missing from the barracks and Louise from the café. Not only so, but the proprietor of the café was anxiously looking for the 10,000 francs which Louise had stolen for the purpose of her unofficial honeymoon.

That was the last we heard of Houssmann, but he certainly succeeded in getting clear away with his little Louise, for the authorities kept very quiet about the affair. If Houssmann had been caught they would soon have told us, so as to discourage any who might be tempted to imitate him. But for weeks afterwards we drank to Houssmann and his girl.

We were able to obtain passes to leave the

barracks and go down to the town fairly frequently. In the town there were the usual "red lamp" establishments where romance could be purchased for a couple of francs. The "goods" at these places were a varied and cosmopolitan lot, but I did not hear of any English girls being on the staff. *Vin rouge* was available, and rows were frequent occurrences, but these were promptly dealt with by a patrol specially detailed for the purpose.

The French, of course, regard these matters in a frank, business-like way which comes as rather a shock to the average Englishman. But there is certainly a good deal in favour of their methods. After all, there is nothing to be gained by pretending that human nature is different from what it is, especially when dealing with a collection of men who are not remarkable for their morality. Certainly the French was the best method so far as the Legion was concerned, for practically every man was desperate, caring nothing for God or man. All the *maisons de tolerance* were under the strictest supervision, medical and otherwise ; and officers, N.C.O.s and men each had their separate establishments. It was sordid, horrible, but at any rate it was organized. I shudder to think what Sousse would have been like if vice had been left to look after itself. Port Said would certainly have been relegated to second place.

The red lamp industry was not without its humorous side. Men would argue for hours about the comparative charms and accomplishments of the ladies, and as often as not these arguments ended in a fight.

On one occasion whilst walking towards the Arab quarter I met one of the most popular girls arrayed in the most overwhelming display of mourning I had ever seen. I would not have believed that there was so much crape in all Africa.

"Hullo, Fifi!" I said. "Lost your husband?"

"No," she answered sedately, "it is my papa who is dead." Then with the usual languishing glance she added the customary remarks about the terrible thirst from which she was suffering, and how I was the one man in all the Legion who really had a place in her heart.

These girls seemed quite happy and contented with their lot. They regarded their trade as a perfectly normal occupation, like domestic service, or working in a factory. They were comparatively well treated and were certainly much better off than the average English outcast. There was

51

nothing furtive about them and they were more non-moral than immoral.

Of course, there was the question of what happened to them when they were old and their charm had faded. But this, according to the average legionnaire, was easily answered. They remained where they were. It was impossible to imagine some of them being older and more faded.

There were times when their lives were somewhat too adventurous to be pleasant.

One night half a dozen legionnaires, all gloriously drunk, were refused admission to one of these establishments for the good and sufficient reason that they had no money. They retaliated by setting the place alight, chasing the girls through the streets and ducking them in the harbour.

For this exploit they received a fortnight in the cells, "with correction", the latter being the official term for a daily flogging.

Then there was Zorab, the Armenian. This beauty had been a brilliant chemist in civil life, but a hopeless moral twist in his character had resulted in his taking refuge in the Legion. Thin-lipped and beady-eyed, there was a decadent cruelty stamped in every line of his features. A student of the works of the Marquis de Sade, he had already got into trouble for kidnapping an Arab girl and mutilating her.

It was the Zorab's boast that he knew the secret of the famous love philtre of the ancient Egyptians, and he was very fond of describing the interesting results he had obtained by trying the stuff on unsuspecting ladies of his acquaintance.

It was this "love philtre", I gathered from his yarns, that was responsible for his presence in the Legion. By way of enlivening a very formal dinner at which a number of eminent scientists with their wives and daughters had been present, he had doped the very respectable wife of his host, with the most scandalous results.

Zorab's stories about his love philtre and his collection of photographs—he claimed that this was the largest and most indecent in the world—made him a very popular member of the Legion, and there were numerous requests for supplies of the magic potion. These, however, were always refused—some said this was because the love philtre existed only in Zorab's imagination.

Soon there were endless arguments between the believers and the scoffers. Everybody agreed that the only way of deciding the matter was to arrange for a practical demonstration. Zorab said that he would be delighted, but unfortunately the ingredients were very expensive indeed and he was a poor man. If his comrades would provide the necessary funds, he would provide the love philtre. A collection having been made and Zorab being satisfied that there was no more cash to be extracted from his comrades—he was suspiciously flush for weeks afterwards—he set to work.

The next question was on whom the experiment should be made. Somebody suggested the Commandant's wife, but this was dismissed as a waste of opportunity. Everybody agreed that it would be better to make a thorough test with the ladies of one of the largest red lamp establishments. Then as many as possible would have a chance of sharing in the fun.

The philtre was duly prepared and carefully introduced into some chocolate creams. One evening the scientific investigators, all armed with doped chocolates, set off to make the great experiment.

From the fuss that was made and the stories that were told, the rest of us gathered that the affair had proved a complete triumph for Zorab. His love philtre possessed all the qualities that he claimed for it.

And several legionnaires decided to take up the study of chemistry when their period of service was over. Meanwhile they had ample time in the cells in which to contemplate the wonders of science.

But romance at Sousse was not wholly a polite term for degradation. There was Houssmann and his little Louise. Who knows? Perhaps they have settled down to contented respectability in some prosperous business bought with the francs which Louise stole from the café.

And there was the Bulgarian who fell in love with the daughter of an Arab trader. He was little more than a boy, quiet, shy and sensitive, and it was a mystery to the rest of us how he came to find himself in the Legion.

His love-affair had all the charm and sweetness of youthful romance. He used to meet the girl by moonlight in the garden of her father's house. He wore a flower which she had given him under his tunic.

Then one night the Bulgarian failed to return to the barracks, and the following day his body was found in the harbour. The truth was never discovered. The Arab trader merely shrugged his shoulders and said that he had never seen the man before. His daughter, he added, had been

given in marriage to a man who lived "beyond
the desert". Whether that really was her fate is
a matter of conjecture. The mystery was never
cleared up, though there was more than a suspicion that the old Arab had at least one murder
to his credit.

The Arab quarter was an amusing place to
visit—provided you had no objection to the smell
of the fragrant East. There was the usual crowd
of merchants, all shouting unintelligibly and all
demanding the most fantastic prices for their
wares. And as usual the prospective purchaser
had only to shake his head and walk away in
order to bring the prices down with a rush. There
were the entertainment touts, too, who in very
confidential tones informed the visitor that through
them admittance could be gained to an alleged
secret establishment where the most marvellous
dancing girls performed the *danse du ventre* and
other oriental delights. The touts, however,
seldom wasted their time over the men of the
Legion. They knew that they had no money.

I make no claim to being a saint, but I avoided
"romance" during my stay at Sousse. My comrades
thought I was very fastidious, but somehow I
could find no attraction in making love to a
girl who had already been mauled about by half

the scum of Europe. I preferred to stick to *vin rouge* as a hobby.

There was a little Spanish girl, however, with whom I became quite good friends. She was nothing like what Spanish girls are supposed to be. Her eyes did not flash and there was no fiery passion about her. She did not click castanets, and, so far as I am aware, she did not carry a dagger in her garter. She was just a plump, homely little soul who was employed in a photographer's shop. Being under the delusion that everybody in England was enormously wealthy, her chief ambition was to go there, and she regarded me as the Heaven-sent means of perfecting her very inadequate knowledge of the language.

She was very excited when she heard that Houssmann had succeeded in escaping with Louise, the waitress at the café, and suggested that we should follow their example. It was a very awkward moment. I had no objection to escaping, but somehow she did not fit in with my idea of a blissfully happy future. On the other hand, I could not be so ungallant as to say so. I agreed, therefore, that it would be splendid, but hinted that Houssmann's success might make the authorities more alert. But she was confident that what had been done once could be done again, and that we could surmount any obstacle. I was greatly relieved a few days later when she told me regretfully that her most unsatisfactory employer did not possess the necessary 10,000 francs for her to steal, and that the project would have to be abandoned.

Apart from drinking and "love making", the favourite diversion was gambling. Poker, banker, "Slippery Sam", and similar games of sheer exciting luck, were the favourites. The owner of a dilapidated roulette wheel did well, too, until the habits of his machine were discovered.

There were some who devoted practically every spare moment they had to the feverish wooing of the goddess of Fortune. Often in an evening a man would lose not only every franc he possessed, but his pay for weeks to come. Some would bet on every possible occasion—on the number of men who would receive a slash with the whip at riding drill—on a race between a couple of lice. Several of the players were more skilful than straight-forward. Arguments and fights were matters of course.

We had been about four months at Sousse when volunteers for the war against the Druses in Syria were called for. Georgia, Whittingham, and I, stepped forward. It was the first that we had heard of the Druses, and I, for one, was not at all sure where Syria was. But we were tired of the monotony of barrack life and were ready to welcome anything in the nature of a change. Besides, a war offered something in the way of excitement.

Unfortunately, Whittingham had an accident soon afterwards. He fell down some stairs and broke his wrist. His name, therefore, had to be removed from the draft.

Christmas day came just before we left Sousse. The Legion is no place for the religiously minded. There are no padres, no church parades, and the three great sects of the British Army—C. of E.s, R.C.s, and "fancy religions"—are unknown. But Christmas is observed with great enthusiasm.

We received presents in the form of pipes and packets of cigarettes. And we had the best meal we had tasted for many a long day. Of course, the fare did not extend to turkey and plum pudding, but we could have as much pork, beans, and potatoes as we could eat. And there were barrels of wine.

The result was that nearly everybody became gloriously drunk, and I shall never forget the sight of a little Jew, full of pork and fuller still of *vin rouge*, standing on the table and singing "Hark, the Herald Angels Sing" at the top of his voice.

Later on there were some equally glorious arguments and fights, and several ended Christmas either in the cells or in hospital. Everybody, however, agreed that it had been a good day.

Being detailed for horse guard, for which I received five francs as extra duty pay, I missed the fun in the evening. But I was so drunk that I made a hopeless mess of the task of watering and feeding the horses. The orderly officer when he came round was in little better condition.

"Legionnaire," he hiccoughed, as he swayed to and fro, "you're drunk !"

"Yes, sir," I agreed, standing to attention with the aid of gripping a horse's tail.

"*Bon !*" was his comment and he staggered on his way.

They were vivid months that we spent at Sousse, fierce and elemental. The heat and the eternal swarms of flies—the cruel discipline—a scream of pain following the sharp crack of a whip—heart-breaking fatigues under the blazing sun—wild, drunken orgies—the solitude of the cells—bestial fights—degradation— Only a Dante could do justice to that inferno of lost souls.

We lived only for the moment ; we had ceased to care what the future might hold for us. Nothing mattered, except the present. At one moment we were snarling, sullen brutes ; at another we were roaring songs at the tops of our voices— but we were still brutes.

We were in the Legion and could sink no lower in the scheme of things. Outcasts, every one of us.

CHAPTER V

O N Boxing Day the draft for Syria received
its orders. We collected our kits and fell
in on the barrack square in full marching
order. There were sixty-six men in the draft,
two sergeants and a lieutenant. I was the only
Englishman, but my friend Georgia was beside me.

We were inspected by the Commandant, and
then each man received the gift provided by the
Society of the Great Ladies of France—two
francs, two packets of cigarettes, half a dozen
oranges, and a bottle of wine.

We could never thank those unknown Great
Ladies who were responsible for that very human
little gift; they belonged to a different world.
But there was not a man who was not affected.
Even the roughest and loneliest amongst us,
calloused in heart and spirit, suddenly realized
that he was not alone in the world after all. He
had found a friend.

63

It was as if a fleeting ray of healing sunshine had broken the dungeon's gloom. The sun remained unseen, but memories of happier days came stealing back. And we could imagine those Great Ladies—sweet, gentle and gracious, like angels of pity.

For a few moments we were men again. We were transformed by the magic touch of charity.

Then the sergeant's voice recalled us to the barrack square and reality. The gifts were stowed away in our kit-bags, and in a few minutes we were marching through the town on our way to the railway station, where we were herded into the inevitable cattle-trucks. A thoroughly tedious and unpleasant journey ended at a small port called Bizert. Here we were confined in barracks for two days with nothing to do but squabble and argue amongst ourselves.

The last reason why any of us had volunteered for the war in Syria was the desire to fight for France, honour and fidelity, and the general idea was to escape at the earliest opportunity. To starving men and desperate fugitives from justice the Legion had seemed a Heaven-sent asylum, but now the position was different. Each believed that he had been cheated. Each was asking himself the question : Why should I throw my life away in this war between France and the Druses? God knows that life had little enough left for most of us, but that little was better than suicide.

Stories were told of the hopeless way in which France was mismanaging this "little war", of the fiendish cruelty of the Druses. There were stories, too, of how the Legion was used merely as cannon fodder. The fiercest hardships and the most dangerous tasks always fell to the Legion, whilst the other troops were held in reserve. Nobody cared how many legionnaires were slaughtered; a fresh supply of cannon fodder could always be obtained from Sousse. Once in the Syrian desert we would not stand a dog's chance.

"Why should we do the dirty work of France?" demanded a big German. "Why should we be the cattle taken to the slaughter house? No, my friends, for myself I jump it."

And with this sentiment most of us agreed. Of course, there were some who pointed out that it was easier to talk of escape than to accomplish it. Many had attempted it, but very few had succeeded, and those who had failed had paid for their rashness either with their lives or with long terms of imprisonment. These, however, were dismissed as obstructive pessimists. If they preferred to be knifed by the Druses and to have their bones left to bleach on the desert, it was their own business.

For my own part, I was fully prepared to make the attempt should a favourable opportunity present itself. I was not forgetting the unfulfilled promises about pay, bonus and promotion, and I considered that I had been badly swindled. There was too much of the "heads I win, tails you lose" in the methods of the French authorities, and I did not consider that agreement to serve France with honour and fidelity in any way binding on my conscience. I did not object to the harsh discipline ; I realized that that was a necessity when dealing with blackguards in the mass. And I had no objection to being called upon to fight against the Druses, or anybody else. Fighting, after all, was the business of the Legion. But I did object to being the victim of cynical and deliberate lying. If I had had a square deal, if I had received the pay and the bonus I had been promised, if there had been a reasonable prospect of my gaining promotion, I would gladly have fulfilled my contract to the letter. As it was, I had no qualms on the question of escaping.

I kept my views to myself, however, realizing that it would be impossible for the whole draft

to escape and that the best chance of success lay
in a quiet solo effort.

After two days of inactivity at Bizert the
authorities indulged in another of those comic
"medical examinations". As usual, it was a
complete farce and could have been successfully
passed by a blind cripple in the last stages of
consumption.

"You are fit?" asked the doctor. "You feel
well? You think you will make good the war?"
And without waiting for an answer, he added:
"Good! Pass on!"

One man, who either possessed a sense of
humour or else did not understand the rules of
the game, protested that he was not feeling at all
fit. Before the doctor could recover from the
shock, the corporal had made it clear to the
culprit with the aid of a kick on the shin
that malingerers were not welcome in the
Legion.

After that, everybody agreed that he felt quite
well, thank you, and hoped to make a very good
war.

This formality completed, we paraded on the
barrack square, were inspected by the Commandant, and finally marched down to the quay.
It was quite a ceremonial affair, with bands

playing and flags flying. A squadron of Moroccan Spahis led the van ; then followed a company of Tirailleurs ; and finally the legionnaires. The populace turned out and cheered enthusiastically —it will be remembered that we had been confined to barracks during our short stay and not let loose on them.

Our transport was a passenger liner, so we travelled in style. And before I had been on board half an hour I discovered that Alexandria was to be our first port of call. I smiled quietly on hearing this. Alexandria was British, and if only I could succeed in slipping ashore I would be able to snap my fingers at the Legion.

I spent most of the voyage turning the idea over in my mind and trying to formulate some definite plan. Then, on the afternoon before we were due to reach Alexandria, the officer in charge of the draft sent for me.

"Harvey," he said, "we're approaching Alexandria, and it occurs to me that you'll probably attempt to escape there, being an Englishman. I propose to put you under lock and key—unless you will give me your word of honour not to make any attempt to escape."

It was a smashing blow to my hopes, but I rather liked the officer. He was a decent fellow, but very hot-tempered. And I appreciated the frankness of his offer.

"I can't give you my word, sir," I said.

He nodded. "Very well. To-night you will sleep in my cabin."

I was given a clean mattress, and slept that night on the floor at the foot of the lieutenant's bed.

When I awoke in the morning the ship had already been berthed by the quay at Alexandria. Above, I could hear all the hum and bustle of a busy port. Chains were rattling, hawsers creaking, orders were being shouted. There were English voices, too !

"You'd like to go on deck for a breath of fresh air ?" asked the lieutenant.

"I should, sir."

"You'll give me your word of honour to make no attempt at escape ?"

Again I hesitated. I was utterly disillusioned and was determined to escape at the earliest opportunity. Within a few yards of me was British soil. Once on the quay I would be safe, for the British authorities would intervene if the lieutenant made any attempt to recapture me. It would be so easy to give my word of honour—and then to break it.

But I rather liked that lieutenant. And it was bewildering to find that, after several months in the Legion, there was somebody who assumed that I had any honour left. I had almost forgotten what it was to be treated like an ordinary human being.

The lieutenant must have guessed my thoughts, for he smiled in a sardonic way.

"Perhaps it's hardly fair to ask you," he said. "You needn't give me your word. I'll let you go on deck handcuffed to a guard."

But I shook my head. I was not going to be paraded as a malefactor. "No, thank you, sir. I'd rather stay here."

"Just as you like," he answered with a shrug of his shoulders.

I spent all the morning and most of the afternoon looking through the papers and magazines which the lieutenant lent me, and in gazing at the very limited view of Alexandria which could be gained through the porthole. It was not very exciting, but at any rate my temporary prison was luxury itself compared with the barrack cells to which I was accustomed.

Suddenly, at about four o'clock in the afternoon, there was a terrific crash on deck which caused the whole vessel to shiver. It was followed by pandemonium—shouts, yells, stampeding feet, the crack of a whip, screams, frenzied orders.

I craned my head out of the porthole, but could see nothing of what was happening. Gradually the turmoil subsided, and matters became normal again.

After a time the lieutenant came into the cabin ; he was obviously in the very worst of tempers. I could not, however, resist the temptation to ask him what had been the cause of the excitement.

"Twenty German legionnaires have escaped, damn them !" he spluttered.

I remembered the long discussions which had taken place in the barrack-rooms at Bizert, and I could not help smiling.

"If you don't take that grin off your face, you'll find yourself in chains !" he roared, emphasizing his remarks with a kick.

It was not until some time later, when a meal was brought down to me, that I was able to learn what had happened.

The German legionnaires had been standing in a group near the gangway, watching the loading and unloading of the cargo. A strong guard of Tirailleurs had been placed near the gangway to prevent any unauthorized person leaving the ship, and they had been threatened with all sorts of pains and penalties if anybody succeeded in getting ashore.

Suddenly the chain of one of the cranes had snapped and a great packing case had crashed on to the deck near the gangway. Fortunately nobody was injured, but the startled guard had scattered, not knowing what was coming next.

Before anybody could realize what was happening the Germans had seized their opportunity. Making a dash for the gangway, they bowled over any bewildered guards who chanced to be in their way and sprinted for the shore.

They were half-way across the quay before the lieutenant, beside himself with rage, appeared on the scene. Lashing blindly out with his riding-whip, the lieutenant elicited yells of pain from guards, crew, dock-hands, and anybody else who had the misfortune to be within range. The guards, grabbing their rifles, dashed off in pursuit of the deserters, only to find their way barred by a British dock policeman, who announced that no armed party could be permitted to land without Government authority.

The lieutenant, after expressing his opinion of the dock policeman, strode off to interview the port officials. By this time, of course, the deserters had long since disappeared from sight and were doubtless making themselves scarce in the narrow streets of Alexandria. In any case, the interview with the port officials did not prove very satisfactory from the lieutenant's point of view, and he returned to the ship in as black a rage as ever. What had happened, apparently, was that he had been politely told that nothing could be done. The men were German nationals and therefore, if they were to be handed over to anybody, it must be to the German and not the French authorities.

In the circumstances, the lieutenant, being responsible for handing over the draft intact at Damascus, may be forgiven for losing his temper. But after the incident a number of people took care to keep as far as possible from him and his riding-whip.

When we had left Alexandria I was allowed on deck again, and the first person I bumped into was a civilian passenger for Jaffa who had come on board at Alexandria. He swore at me in English and I returned the compliment.

"—— !" he exclaimed, stretching out his hand. "Are you English ?"

"I am," I admitted.

"Then come and have a spot with me !" he said, leading the way to his cabin.

He was not, perhaps, very edifying company and he was not altogether sober. But it was good to hear an English voice again. And it was good to taste Scotch whisky again after the *vin rouge* to which I had become accustomed. He had brought a whole caseful to fortify himself for the voyage. He disdained anything in the nature of soda-water and just poured it neat down his throat. It was not long before we were the best of friends.

He was not very communicative about himself, but he was obviously the black sheep of some good family—a remittance man, probably. Even when drunk he was still the public schoolboy. Apparently he had some sort of a job, for he said that he was going to Jaffa on business. But his chief occupation was drinking himself to death.

Poor devil! Perhaps he had only himself to thank for it; perhaps he was just another of Fate's broken playthings. Who knows?

As we approached Port Said I was again locked up in the lieutenant's cabin. On this occasion, evidently, he was leaving nothing to chance, for I was not asked if I would give my word of honour to make no attempt to escape.

The lieutenant's task, however, was not an easy

one. The ship was not a transport, but a passenger
and cargo boat. I would not like to say whether
the legionnaires would be described as passengers
or cargo, but the lieutenant could not do exactly
as he liked. And it was no concern of the skipper's
if the whole Legion escaped. He had enough
worries of his own. Moreover, relations between
the two hadn't been any too cordial since the whip-
cracking exhibition at Alexandria.

It was late in the afternoon when we reached
Port Said, and for several hours I had nothing to
do but sit in the cabin and listen to the sounds
on deck.

Suddenly there was a terrific uproar. A few
minutes later a very excited sergeant burst into
the cabin and loudly demanded to know where
the lieutenant was.

"He hasn't been here for an hour, or more," I
answered. "What's the trouble, sergeant ?"

"Ten more swine have escaped !" he said.
"There will be the devil to pay !"

There was. A moment later the lieutenant
came striding into the cabin, black as thunder.
And before the sergeant could say a word
he had felled him with a terrific blow on the
jaw.

Not being on the look-out for trouble, I

withdrew discreetly to a corner of the cabin and developed a sudden interest in a French newspaper.

Again I had to wait a considerable time before I could learn the details.

It was a mixed crowd of Russians, Poles, Serbs, and Germans who had escaped. They had been lounging about the deck in twos and threes, laughing and chatting and taking very good care not to allow anybody to guess that they had a concerted plan of escape.

As darkness fell they edged their way nearer and nearer to the guard which had been mounted over the gangway. Suddenly one of the Germans had cried: "Look!" and pointed excitedly towards the shore. Naturally, the unsuspecting guards had looked. And at the same instant the Russians, the Poles, and the Serbs had set upon them, taking them completely by surprise. Whilst the guards were picking themselves up and sorting themselves out, the ten deserters were busy sprinting for the dock gates.

The lieutenant had ordered the guard to fire on the escaping men, but a port official who happened to be on deck warned him that this would mean his instant arrest, the ship being in British waters.

The much-tried officer had thereupon rushed below to "let off steam" on the unfortunate sergeant, who was in no way responsible for the affair, and subsequently on the equally unfortunate Tirailleurs who had been on guard.

Having absolutely no chance of escaping myself, I could not help feeling rather sorry for the lieutenant who, after all, was quite a decent fellow in ordinary circumstances. He had already lost thirty of his draft of sixty-six and would undoubtedly have to face some very awkward questions at the end of the voyage.

What actually happened to him I never heard, but it was quite possible that he was court-martialled. In any case, I am sure that during that voyage he became convinced that it was no joke being an officer in the Foreign Legion.

Our next port of call was Jaffa, and before being locked up again I received a parting gift from my new friend in the shape of a half-bottle of whisky. He had drunk all the rest of the case, and remarked that it was not worth taking any ashore with him, as he would soon be able to get a fresh supply.

Special precautions were taken to prevent any further escapes. Double guards were placed on the gangways and all troops were confined to the lower deck. N.C.O.s were constantly moving about on the watch for any hint of trouble.

Even the lieutenant was satisfied that it was impossible for him to lose any more of his draft at Jaffa.

I was sitting in the cabin gazing through the porthole at the scene on shore, when I heard a splash. It was followed by several more. And a moment later I saw five men swimming frantically towards the dock.

The usual pandemonium broke out on deck. Shouts, screams, curses, and above the din the lieutenant yelling incoherently and cracking his riding-whip.

As at Port Said the guards dared not open fire on the deserters, for we were in British waters. An attempt, I gathered afterwards, was made to lower a boat and go in pursuit, but in the excitement it got jammed. Anyhow, I saw the five scramble ashore like half-drowned terriers and, with a gesture of jeering triumph at the boat, disappear from sight.

That made thirty-five missing—more than half the draft !

I have often wondered what happened to the "lucky" ones. They had no passports and were

utterly destitute ; many of them could not speak
a word of English. Perhaps they were handed
over to the care of their Consuls. Perhaps they
were arrested by the British authorities and
deported to their native countries as undesirable
aliens. The latter would have been a hard fate
for the Russians, for they were all refugees from
the Bolshevists.

At the time, however, I was chiefly concerned
with wondering when the lieutenant would return
to his cabin. Remembering the sergeant's
experience at Port Said, I was anything but
anxious to meet him and bear the brunt of his
anger.

The ship was under way when at last he did
come striding into the cabin. He was still livid
with rage and he still had his riding-whip in his
hand. I said nothing and did my best to look
very good and sympathetic. At the same time I
fully expected to receive the lash of the whip
across my shoulders.

"Get to hell out of this !" he roared.

I wasted no time in getting. I just bolted.

A few days later we reached Beyrout, the
principal port of Syria, and the end of our voyage.
We were roused early, and as we paraded on deck
in full marching order we saw the sun rise from

behind the mountains of Lebanon with their olive groves and wooded slopes.

On disembarking, we were inspected by the local Commandant and then, with the Spahis and Tirailleurs who had been our fellow passengers, were marched to barracks behind a drum-and-fife band. I don't know what subsequently happened to the Tirailleurs and Spahis, but the Foreign Legion draft, or what was left of it, was placed under an armed guard. This, possibly, was the result of the number of desertions which had taken place during the voyage. Or perhaps the Commandant, having had legionnaires under his temporary care before, believed in playing for safety.

In any case, I objected to being treated as if I were a prisoner. After my enforced good conduct on the voyage, too, I was feeling ready for any sort of adventure. I wanted to let off the steam which had been accumulating during all the hours I had sat locked in the lieutenant's cabin with nothing to do but realize that I was within a dozen yards of British territory—if only I could reach it. Of course, Beyrout being in the hands of the French, it was hopeless to attempt to escape from there, but it occurred to me that a stroll round the town was likely to be more attractive than sitting in a bare barrack-room.

My friend Georgia also found inactivity irksome. He was one of the few members of the draft who had no desire to escape; he still believed that some day he would win a commission. Besides, escape had nothing to offer him.

But enforced idleness always had a maddening effect upon him. It left him with nothing to do but think, and all he asked of life was to forget. For hour after hour, he strode up and down that barrack-room, his fists clenched and a scowl on his face.

The others jeered and laughed at him in their brutish way, but my heart was aching for him. I knew that he was thinking of the old days when he had been a prince and a captain in the body-guard of the Czar. I could see that he was enduring again those days of horror when he had been stripped of everything, when his wife and kiddies had been butchered.

"How about breaking out of barracks and having a look round the town?" I suggested as soon as darkness had fallen.

"Right you are!" he agreed.

Luck was with us. We managed to dodge the guards while they were being changed and, meeting nobody, escaped from the barracks by climbing over the wall. Going down towards the docks, it was not long before we found a low-down drinking den.

There was a tough-looking crowd present, mostly sailors, from the look of them, and a few girls. One of the latter immediately took a fancy to Georgia and came over and joined us. I thought at first that there was going to be trouble, but the men contented themselves with scowling at us.

Georgia had plenty of money on him and it was not long before the *vin rouge* industry was booming. It was a real mad binge ; we were determined to get drunk as quickly as possible ; we did not care what happened. We had broken out of barracks and were bound to get into trouble ; we were going to make the most of our freedom. Georgia was in the wildest of moods. The girl, too, was a dark-haired, laughing-eyed witch, ready for any devilry.

The more we drank the wilder we became. We sang songs at the tops of our voices. A couple of glasses were broken. A crowd began to gather. Finally the proprietor refused to serve us with any more drink. There was every prospect of there being a real rough house.

Then the girl linked her arms in ours and told

us that if we went with her we could get all the drink we wanted.

I was very drunk. In a foggy sort of way I was conscious of walking along a street, of being in a room, of more wine, of watching Georgia kissing and cuddling the girl who was sitting on his knee. At last it sank in to my befuddled brain that it was a case where two were company and three none. I rose to my feet, expressed eternal friendship for Georgia and the girl, and, by the grace of providence, succeeded in staggering back to barracks.

It was half-past two in the morning. Needless to say, there was trouble with a capital T. The draft was to parade at four o'clock and start for Damascus ; our absence had been discovered, and there had been a lot of excitement. The guards who had allowed us to escape had been put under arrest ; the police had been notified ; patrols had been sent out to look for us.

Fortunately for me, the briefness of our stay at Beyrout made it impossible for full disciplinary action to be taken, otherwise I should undoubtedly have got it properly "in the neck". As it was, there was only time for the sergeant to tell me his very candid opinion of me and my parentage. Never have I heard a man swear more fluently or more forcefully. He was a Russian, and life in the Legion had made him something of a linguist. Every cuss word in every European language was included in his repertoire.

Blissfully drunk, I swayed and listened to him with smiling admiration.

I stopped smiling, however, when I heard the whistle of his whip and felt the stinging thong curling round my shoulders. I just fled in the direction of my quarters.

The return of Georgia, very much the worse for wear, shortly after three o'clock, resulted in another outburst of international obscenity and blasphemy.

Anybody else would probably have kicked and flogged us into sobriety, but that sergeant never forgot that Georgia was a fellow countryman and once had been a prince and a captain in the Czar's bodyguard. He would swear at him with hair-raising ferocity, but he never struck him. It was his way of showing that he was still loyal to the old régime.

Having more or less sobered ourselves with the aid of a bucket of water, Georgia and I scrambled on parade. It was soon evident that serious business was on foot and that we were nearing the end of our journey to the front. Every man

84

was served out with full field equipment, including a ".tin hat" and 250 rounds of ammunition. We had also to carry rifles in addition to our sabres. In fact, so far as appearances went, it was difficult to say whether we were cavalry or infantry.

In due course we were marched down to the station and boarded a ramshackle train. Georgia and I promptly settled down to a much-needed sleep. This, however, was by no means easy. The engine was old and infirm ; the track was in a terrible state ; and the cattle-trucks were innocent of springs. The result was that we proceeded in a series of jolts and bumps, calculated to make sleep impossible. The fact that we and our equipment were overcrowded did not improve matters either.

After a time Georgia and I gave it up as a bad job and came to the conclusion that it was more restful to stand than to sit on the hard floor of the truck.

We had now reached a wild, uncultivated country, strewn with boulders and dotted with olive trees. Within the whole horizon there was not a sign of human habitation to break the dreary monotony of the scene, which had probably remained unaltered since the days of the Bible.

I was lighting a cigarette when, with startling suddenness, a band of tribesmen, hidden among the olive trees and the boulders, opened fire on us. Bullets crashed through the woodwork of the trucks; from the carriages behind us came the sound of splintering glass; screams rang out. Two legionnaires sank choking to the floor, their hands clutching at their blood-stained uniforms.

Flinging ourselves down on the floor, we thrust our rifles through the slats of the trucks and opened fire. An old, half-forgotten thrill came back to me as I pressed a clip of cartridges home in the magazine, closed the bolt and, glancing along the sights at a white-robed figure lurking among the olive trees, pressed the trigger. I was in action again!

The engine-driver, apparently, had been waiting for this moment to open his throttle. Snorting and roaring, the old engine broke into a desperate gallop, with the train clattering and swaying along behind it. It was sheer good luck that the outfit remained on the rails.

For five minutes the miniature battle continued. Flashes spat at us from the rocks and trees. Bullets whined overhead; splinters darted from the woodwork. The train jolted and bumped on its way. Peering through the slats, we emptied clip after clip into the panorama of rocks, trees, sand, and distant white-robed figures which was sliding past us like a film.

Then at length the bandits were left behind and all became quiet again. The train settled down to its former jog-trot.

When we reached Damascus, it was found that the casualties were three dead and four wounded, all the dead being civilian passengers. Two at least of the killed might have been saved if there had been medical attention available on the train.

The authorities, however, were quite satisfied, saying that it was a great improvement on the last affair when the casualties had amounted to seventy, including more than twenty soldiers. On that occasion the engine-driver had been killed and the train had covered several kilos before a civilian managed to crawl along to the footplate and take charge.

These attacks on trains were a fairly frequent occurrence in Syria. The bandits often numbered three hundred or more, and were armed with up-to-date rifles and automatic pistols in addition to their knives. The raids seemed to have been carried out more or less with impunity, and the defence was left in the hands of such troops as happened to be travelling by the train. Generally, the raiders contented themselves with firing on the trains and keeping at a safe distance. But sometimes matters became more serious.

The most sensational raid had taken place some three months previous to our arrival. The train on that occasion was carrying arms, ammunition, and rations, in addition to drafts for the front. Moreover, there was a truck carrying an armoured car and a "75" gun. The news must have reached the bandits in good time, for quite five hundred took part in the raid.

The raiders opened with a terrific fusillade and then, leaping on to their horses, charged upon the train as it lumbered along. The troops shot down scores, but the tribesmen swarmed on to the train. Some, knife in hand, clambered into the carriages and trucks where desperate struggles took place. Others climbed on to the wagons and flung the loot out on to the line.

When the train at last reached Damascus there were more than a hundred and fifty dead and wounded on board. Two hundred rifles, fifteen thousand rounds of ammunition, and ten thousand francs' worth of rations were missing. The entire gun-crew of ten men on the "75" had been wiped out, all by stabbing.

Of course, there was a lot of talk about what

ought to be done to prevent these raids, but the difficulties were practically insuperable. It would have needed an army to hunt down those few hundred elusive tribesmen. It would have needed another army to guard effectively the hundreds of miles of track through the desolate country. The only thing to be done was to hope for the best and be thankful that it had not occurred to the bandits to pull up a length of line and derail the trains. Meanwhile, railway travelling in Syria was not a popular form of amusement, and there was no demand for excursions to the coast from Damascus.

On our arrival we were marched to the citadel. This ancient fortress covers an immense area and dominated the whole town. The courtyard alone is large enough to take six regiments of cavalry.

The citadel is the grimmest-looking building that ever I have seen. Like a bloated giant it scowls malignly on the world, gloating over the shudders it inspires. Inside, it is a rabbit-warren of cells, dungeons, torture chambers, oubliettes, and secret passages, a temple of terror which has endured through centuries. Every stone hints at some tale of ghastly horror. The Arabs say that devils live there. And even now people talk in whispers of the terrible things that happen in Damascus citadel.

Even the legionnaires, hardened and soulless as they were, could not escape the baleful atmosphere of the place. There were no ribald songs or jokes. Even the sergeants cursed in an undertone.

We did not fail to notice, however, that the town possessed other features besides the citadel. There were cafés which looked invitingly luxurious; and there were smartly-dressed European ladies, the wives of French officers, to be seen. After the arid wilderness through which we had passed, Damascus seemed comparable with Paris or London.

"I think we shall have to indulge in an evening off whilst we're here," remarked Georgia. "It looks an interesting sort of place."

I agreed, and we accordingly took the earliest opportunity for asking for a couple of passes. Georgia acted as spokesman and told the usual tale about our interest in antiquities and our anxiety to inspect the famous old city. Our application, however, was curtly refused.

An attempt to break out resulted only in my getting a couple of slashes with a whip, and we spent our evening in Damascus playing banker in a drab barrack-room. We hadn't even a bottle of *vin rouge* to enliven us.

When we turned in for the night we decided that, no matter what happened, we would explore Damascus on the morrow.

At dawn, however, we were roused and warned that we were to parade within half an hour. And after our meagre meal of coffee and bread we were marched back to the railway station and herded into the inevitable cattle-trucks.

There followed an interminable journey across mile after mile of sun-scorched wilderness. The train creaked and clattered and jolted along the single line of badly-laid track. There was nothing to do, nothing to see. Rest was impossible. We could only curse the heat, the flies, each other, and our own aching bones.

On and on we jolted through eternal desolation.

Then at last, with much bumping and clanging, the train drew up.

We had reached Mesmie, the desert outpost which was our destination. This was the front !

Now for *la bonne guerre* !

CHAPTER VI

MESMIE

THE front in Syria was very different from the front we used to know in France and Flanders. There were no shell-holes or mine craters, no trenches and no dumps, no ruined farmhouses or shattered trees. There was only the desolation of the desert.

Mesmie, which had been described to us as a "strong point", was a collection of mud huts grouped around an oasis consisting of a water-hole and a few palms. The "fortifications" comprised a ring of rather dilapidated trenches, an equally dilapidated moat, about four feet wide, and a straggling barbed wire entanglement, plentifully ornamented with bully beef tins.

After my experiences in France I considered myself something of a judge of barbed wire entanglements and, frankly, I did not like the look of that Mesmie effort. Any normally able-bodied man could have jumped it, whilst half a dozen could easily have rooted the whole lot up in twenty minutes. As a defence, the thing was ridiculous. It would not have held up a company of boy scouts.

As I discovered later the lack of barbed wire was only typical of the general mismanagement. There was never enough of anything. The ammunition was nearly all old War stock, and contained a large proportion of faulty material. In one machine-gun belt of two hundred and fifty rounds I have known there to be no less than fifty duds—not a very cheerful experience when each dud means a jamb and some hundreds of yelling tribesmen are charging at you !

The equipment was much too heavy for the light Arab horses with which we were supplied. Our uniforms were made of the very worst shoddy and our boots were chiefly remarkable for the amount of cardboard they contained. We were always short of underclothing, with the result that vermin were our constant companions, and a clean shirt could only be obtained by washing your one and only and putting it on whilst it was still wet. Medical supplies were deficient and there was no medical officer nearer than Damascus. For doctoring we had to rely upon the medical corporal, whose only qualifications for the post were a sublime faith in castor oil as a cure for all complaints, and the fact that before joining the Legion he had poisoned his wife for the sake of the insurance money.

At Mesmie, I often called to mind the old chorus: "Oh, oh, oh, it's a lovely war!" and I decided that the old one was not so bad after all.

In Syria we did not even know what the war was about. Our information was confined to the fact that we were fighting the Druses, who were particularly fierce opponents, never taking any prisoners and with an unpleasant habit of killing the wounded. Undoubtedly they were very cruel, but they were a fine race. Tall, handsome, proud and intelligent, they were very far from being savages. It was said, though I cannot say with what truth, that their god was a golden calf, the same Baal that is mentioned in the Bible. It may be, of course, that they are the descendants of the enemies of the ancient Israelites.

These, however, were questions with which we were not concerned. It was not for us to wonder why France could not leave these people in peace in their native desert. Our job was to kill as many of them as possible before they succeeded in killing us.

Immediately on our arrival we were paraded

before the captain who was in command of the "fort". He was a fine, soldierly man of about sixty, a splendid officer, and absolutely fearless. As will be learnt later he had one terrible twist in his character. In the excitement of battle he was apt to "see red", and in that condition was capable of the most hideous atrocities. Possibly that was the reason why he found himself in command of a lonely desert outpost instead of in some more comfortable position in France. In any case, I would sooner serve under him than any other officer in the world. He was a great leader and a great fighter.

He inspected us very keenly and asked every man his nationality.

"So you are English, eh?" he said to me. "Why did you volunteer for the war in Syria? Was it to fight, or in the hope of escaping into Palestine?"

Naturally, I answered that it was my intention to fight.

He nodded. "You are the first Englishman I have had here. I fought with the English in the Great War, and I know their courage. I shall expect you to set an example to the others. You will be in Number 1 Post, where I can keep an eye on you."

With this cryptic remark I was dismissed and handed over to Corporal Toschinko, a Cossack, who introduced me to my new home—a mud hut with a plank bed, and a roof like a sieve.

"What happens when it rains?" I asked him.

"It just comes in," he answered. "You'll soon see." He added that I would be on guard from midnight until two o'clock, and that Number 1 Post was regarded as a regular death-trap—it had already been wiped out by the enemy on several occasions.

With this cheerful information I turned in and slept until evening. I then wandered round the camp, which was about as large as a football field and garrisoned by 180 men.

At midnight I donned my tin hat and great coat and mounted guard.

There were ten sentries on duty. On my right a big German marched up and down with all the precision of a Prussian Guardsman. On my left there was a forlorn Swiss boy of not more than eighteen. After a time we began to talk in whispers and it was not long before he confided his story to me.

As usual it was a girl who was responsible for his downfall. The boy had become hopelessly infatuated with a rider in a travelling circus, had stolen 50,000 francs from his employer, and run off with his charmer to Marseilles. So long as the money had lasted the girl had been everything that was loving and delightful. But when the last franc had been spent she went off with another man. In despair, the boy had joined the Legion.

Suddenly our conversation was interrupted by a burst of hideous laughter. It sobbed and gurgled through the darkness like the mirth of some fiend incarnate. I stood petrified; never had I heard anything so blood-curdling. My hair rose on my scalp; cold shivers ran down my spine.

"My God! What's that?" I gasped.

"It's only the hyenas," replied the Swiss. "They're starting up for the evening."

Before long a regular hellish symphony was in progress. Hyena answered hyena, jackal howled to jackal, and every other animal of the desert joined in the chorus. For half an hour the hideous din continued. Then it ceased as suddenly as it had started and again there was silence.

Alone in the darkness I paced up and down my beat. Not a sound broke the stillness of the night. My thoughts began to wander.

What was that?

The clanking of tin—a stealthy footfall—the creaking of the wire——

I pictured a Druse crawling up to the wire, stealthily cutting it, creeping towards me, knife in hand! In a few moments he would spring upon me—I would feel the blade as it plunged deep——

Gripping my rifle, I waited.

Again the jingling of a tin in the wire. Judging the spot as best I could, I fired.

The report shattered the night like a cannon. The Swiss cried: *"Qui va la?"* in a shrill voice and I heard his bayonet rattle as he came on guard. Lights showed in the huts. Men were shouting.

A Verey light soared up into the darkness, burst, and illuminated the desert with a blaze of light. The tall black palms, like shadows—the camp—the mud huts——

There on the wire my victim lay dead—a pariah dog!

I never heard the last of that dog.

We soon settled down to life in the desert post. The enemy being quiet and out of sight, so far as we were concerned, it was rather a dull war. There were no aeroplanes to drop bombs on us or artillery to send us an occasional "Black

Johnson". We had little to do beyond lounge about the camp, curse the flies and stare at the desert. We just yawned and waited for something to happen.

The first evidence we had that there was really a war on was one morning a few days after our arrival, when a band of wild-looking Bedouins, clad in flowing burnouses with coloured turbans, came galloping into camp with a French officer at their head. They had rifles slung across their shoulders and in their belts were pistols and wicked-looking knives.

And each man carried a bunch of human heads slung by the hair to his saddle-bow. These grisly trophies had evidently been recently captured, for the horses were all spattered with blood.

These were Bedouin irregulars, and they were paid, I was told, a hundred francs for every Druse head they collected. They were bound by no discipline and acted entirely on their own initiative. From the look of them, I should say that they would have been equally ready to help the Druses —if the latter had offered a fair price for French heads.

During the short time they were with us we were practically confined to our mud huts. This was partly because the Bedouins were very suspicious lest we should try to steal their heads, and partly because they regarded all the regular troops as blackleg labour. An incautious word or action might easily have resulted in a free fight with several funerals to follow.

The officer in charge of them, a French lieutenant, was one of the most remarkable men I have ever seen. He was short and thick-set, with jet-black hair and beard. His voice was like a rasp and his eyes glittered like burning coals. Even in repose his hand was never far from/ the butt of the revolver in his belt. To glance at him was to feel the power of his fierce and dominating personality. Even those wild head-hunters went in awe of him.

They were welcome to him, for it must have been hell to serve under him. Probably there was more than a streak of madness in his composition ; certainly he was not normal. But I wondered then, and have often wondered since, where that over-whelming personality would have taken him if he had not been condemned by Fate to be an officer in the French colonial army. I could see him as a great financier, or the leader of a revolution, like Lenin. Obviously, the Army was the wrong career for him. He was a great leader, but it was easy to guess how intolerable his superiors found him and how glad they had been to sidetrack him as the leader of these Bedouin head-hunters.

Another irregular force assisting the French in Syria were the Cherkes, who were Cossack rough-riders. They were picturesque figures in their fur caps, flowing cloaks, and high boots. They were armed to the teeth with carbine and sword, with a regular arsenal of knives, pistols, and ammunition. They were wonderful horsemen, absolutely fearless and as ferocious as tigers.

A charge by the Cherkes could only be described as a thunderbolt. The Druses were equally good horsemen and equally fierce. A clash between the two was one of the most wonderful and thrilling sights that warfare can provide. It was just a whirling storm of horses, men, flashing swords and stabbing knives, the choking cloud of up-flung sand spattered with darting tongues of flame from revolver and pistol. Then, the two forces having passed through each other, the survivors could be seen wheeling and reforming whilst riderless horses galloped wildly across the desert leaving behind them the dead and dying.

About a week after my arrival at Mesmie, I was selected to form one of a patrol of ten men under a lieutenant and a sergeant, which was sent to visit a distant Arab village. The ride across the desert was uneventful, and the village, when we got there, did not seem a very inviting sort of place.

I had just finished grooming my horse and was wondering how we should fill in our time until we moved off again the following morning, when the lieutenant sent for me.

"There's an Arab chief here who speaks English," he said. "He was educated at one of your public schools. The last time I met him he asked me if we had any Englishmen with us. Would you care to come along and see him?"

Of course I said that I should, and off we went.

The chief was not at home but had gone off to a house nearby to inspect some slaves who were for sale. We accordingly went along to the house where the sale was being held. When we arrived we found seven solemn-looking Arab chiefs watching the posturings and antics of a dozen dancing girls. The music consisted of strumming on a couple of stringed instruments accompanied by the monotonous thumping on a sort of drum. The alleged musicians were apparently completely indifferent to the proceedings and just plugged along with their jobs in a mechanical sort of way.

The dancing was as dull as the music. There was nothing of the thrilling Eastern sensuousness which I had read about in stories. With a set grin on their faces the girls twisted and postured in a lackadaisical way—it reminded me of a lot of schoolgirls "doing their bit" at the annual display. The chiefs stroked their beards and looked bored. The only person who seemed to be enjoying himself was the man who, I gathered, was the auctioneer. He apparently enjoyed every moment of the performance and was convinced that those dancing girls were worth their weight in gold.

The music and the dancing stopped abruptly and the girls, still smiling mechanically, stood in a row. The chiefs stroked their beards and muttered amongst themselves. The auctioneer started to talk.

Whether any sale was effected I had no chance of discovering, for the English-educated chief had noticed the lieutenant and came across to us. He was a tall, handsome man, dressed in a flowing white robe.

The moment he spoke I knew that the lieutenant had been right when he said that the chief had been educated in an English public school. His accent was perfect.

He was delighted when he heard that I was English, and insisted on my accompanying him to his "humble home", as he called it. The home proved to be the nearest approach to a palace that ever I had visited. I found myself in a great room hung with tapestries, and ornamented with swords, pistols and shields, some of them studded with jewels. Sounding a gong, my host ordered wine and cigarettes to be brought.

It must have been several years since the chief had been in England, but he took a very keen interest in affairs there. He asked me innumerable questions about the cricket championship, the university boat race, the plays that were running, the changes that were taking place in London, the Derby, and such-like matters. He also asked me a number of questions about myself and went on to discuss the War, coal-mining, and the Legion. But he refused to tell me anything about himself.

"That's a question I never answer," he said when I asked him the name of the school where he had been educated. "I had a very thin time when I first went there—I was ostracized because I was a 'nigger'. But I won through and found some of the best friends that ever a man had. The memories of those old days are a secret which I treasure in my heart, but never mention to an outsider."

"Will you ever go back to England?" I asked.

He smiled and shrugged his shoulders. "I doubt it. My place is here. Besides, what would my friends say if I were suddenly to turn up with my eight wives?"

"Eight wives?" I echoed. Somehow, it seemed incredible that this product of an English public school, who, but a few moments ago, had been talking about cricket, should have eight wives.

"Yes, would you like to see them?"

I accepted the invitation and we went along to the harem, which was guarded by a big negro armed with a two-edged sword.

The chief summoned his wives by clapping his hands. They were all heavily veiled from head to foot and all that could be seen of them was their eyes. So far as could be judged, they all seemed to have very fine figures.

They filed past us and the chief introduced me to each in turn. I bowed and noted how their eyes twinkled and gleamed. It was a tantalizing situation and, being unable to see them, I was sure that those girls were the prettiest on earth.

"Can't they take their veils off so that I can see their faces?" I asked.

If I had dropped a bomb the effect could not have been more startling. The chief forgot all about being an English public schoolboy and stormed at me in his own language. The wives stood huddled together. The negro gripped his sword.

Not being sure what was going to happen next, I made sure that I had my revolver handy.

After a time, however, the chief quietened down, and with a wave of his hand dismissed his wives.

"Never seek to see the faces of our women," he said as we walked away. "It is forbidden for infidels to look upon the faces of Allah's chosen."

After this the interview was inclined to flag and it was not long before I departed, the chief calling me "brother" and calling upon Allah to protect me.

"How did you get on?" asked the lieutenant afterwards.

He nodded when I told him of the chief's outburst on the subject of his wives' faces. "His civilization is a very thin veneer," he said. "It's a pose more than anything else, and he keeps it up chiefly because he hopes to obtain special favours from us."

When I told some of my comrades of the

incident it was suggested that we should break into the chief's harem and see for ourselves whether those wives were good-lookers or not. I think, incidentally, that some of them were also interested in the chief's collection of jewelled swords. Fortunately, however, the patrol had to move on before this bright idea could be put into operation.

On our return to Mesmie I was appointed batman to the captain. I jumped at the chance, remembering the old days when it was everybody's ambition to get attached to company headquarters. I had to clean up the captain's hut, polish his equipment, and generally look after him. I missed the ordinary fatigues, but had to take my turn at guard duty.

It was certainly very much better than having nothing to do most of the day but lounge about the camp. And the captain's company was to be preferred to that of most of my comrades. He was tremendously energetic and scrupulously just to the men under him. His one great fault, as will be seen later, was his habit of seeing red when in action. In normal moments he was splendid.

So far as the difference in our stations allowed, the captain and I became the best of friends.

Living in such isolated and cramped conditions as those which obtained at Mesmie, it was inevitable that officers, N.C.O.s, and men should fraternize on a scale which would have seemed fantastic in barracks. And, probably as a result of the training we had had at Sousse, discipline in no way suffered. The captain's word was absolute.

For some time nothing happened and we began to wonder whether the Druses had forgotten us. We were not exactly anxious that they should pay us a visit. On the other hand, we were utterly and completely fed up with our monotonous existence in the desert outpost.

Our chief occupation was "grousing". We grumbled at the heat, the flies, the desert, and each other. And especially we grumbled at the Director of Ordnance at Damascus, whose chief object in life was apparently to keep us short of supplies. The captain sent indent after indent, but something always seemed to go wrong. If he asked for socks it was more than likely that we received bully beef. The worst scandal of all was the way in which we were starved of ammunition. In spite of the fact that the post had been the scene of desperate fighting, and in spite of the captain's representations, we had only sufficient for one day's hard fighting—and of that an unknown proportion was dud.

Apart from the Frenchman's natural aptitude for mismanagement, this niggardliness was in great part deliberate. The official view was that the Foreign Legion did not really matter; fresh supplies of cannon fodder could always be obtained from Sousse.

We had been awaiting a train with supplies for several days when one morning an aeroplane circled low over the camp and dropped a packet containing a message and a couple of sacks of bully beef and biscuits. The message was to the effect that a column of Druses had been seen heading in our direction and that we could expect to be attacked. It added that the railway line had been cut, but it was hoped to get a train through shortly.

No information as to when we might expect the enemy or as to their numbers. And no attempt to provide us with the much-needed ammunition which the captain had been clamouring for.

With the line cut behind us we were practically trapped in the desert. We had rations enough for a week; a day's hard fighting would see the end of our ammunition. It was not a cheerful prospect.

The captain might have phoned through to Damascus to point out our plight and to urge that a train should be sent through as soon as possible, but we dared not use the telephone for important communications. Many of the telephone operators, railway, and other officials were spies working for the Druses, always on the lookout for useful information to pass on to the enemy. To have phoned through to headquarters would in all probability have sealed our fate. Learning that we were short of ammunition, the enemy would have overwhelmed us.

In Damascus, so I was told, there were hundreds of the Druses' secret agents. Their work was rendered all the easier by the fact that the natives hated the French and looked to the Druses to deliver them.

That night double sentries were posted. Our only visitors, however, were the jackals and hyenas.

No train arrived, and no further news. Two long days passed in tense expectation.

On the third night I was on guard from ten until midnight. There was something eerie in the silence. Not a star shone to break the darkness. The palms stood like dim shadows against the black vault of the heavens.

Those were the longest two hours I have ever known. Gripping my rifle, I stood peering into the darkness, my ears straining to catch the slightest sound. In my imagination I could see the enemy creeping nearer and nearer to the wire.

Nothing happened, and at midnight I went off duty. I found the captain striding up and down the hut. Like the rest of us, he was feeling the strain and found sleep impossible. There was no escape from the great questions: When would the enemy attack? Would they come in hundreds, or thousands? Would we be able to hold out until further supplies arrived? How long was this nerve-racking suspense to last? What was to happen within the next twenty-four hours?

In all war there is nothing worse that that period of inaction which precedes an attack. It is then, when you have nothing to do but think and wonder, that you plumb the depths of human experience. It is life at its worst.

The captain sent me off to serve out a ration of rum to the men. He had been drinking heavily himself, but in those conditions of nervous strain drink has little or no effect. Indeed, it seems to sober a man.

I went round the posts, serving each man with

a pannikin of rum. Needless to say, I received a warm welcome. There had been none of the old carousals since our arrival at Mesmie, for the very good reason that it had been impossible for us to obtain anything more than our ration of *vin rouge*, and that issue of rum made even an attack by the Druses worth while. Never have I been wished good health with more enthusiasm or in more languages.

The night crept on, but still nothing happened. We began to hope that dawn and the supply train would reach us before the Druses attacked.

Then, at about two o'clock in the morning, a shot rang out with startling suddenness. Another —another—hoarse shouts——

Grabbing my rifle and equipment I rushed to the captain's hut. He was buckling three pistols in his belt.

"Come on, Harvey!" he cried. "The swine are here at last! Come on!"

He was utterly different from his normal bluff self. His lips were twisted and there was a curious glitter in his eyes. Even in my excitement I could not help noticing it. There was madness in that gleam.

As we hurried across to the trenches the very atmosphere of the camp seemed to have changed.

The period of suspense was over at last. The enemy were here. All was tense with excitement.

Within a few moments of the alarm being given every man was at his post. There was neither flurry not panic.

A Verey light shot upwards and illuminated the desert with its ghostly glare, revealing dozens of white lumps crawling towards the wire.

Instantly the rifles spat and flashed all along the line. Some of the enemy rose to their feet and hurled themselves headlong upon the wire. Others seized their rifles and returned our fire.

The attack developed swiftly. Within a few moments of the first warning shot it had attained the fury of a tornado.

Verey lights hissed upwards. The Druses flung themselves upon the wire, frenziedly hacking and tearing at it like demons. As fast as they were shot down, others pressed forward in their places. Death meant nothing to them.

We fired as fast as we could manipulate the bolts of our rifles, pressing clip after clip into the magazine. Bullets whistled overhead and spattered against the walls of the mud huts behind us. Men sank to the ground cursing and choking. Machine-guns stuttered and rattled. And still those white figures clawed and wrenched at the tangled strands of rusty barbed wire which alone prevented us from being overwhelmed by sheer weight of numbers.

Scores fell writhing across the wire. Scores more rose up out of the darkness and pressed forward.

Suddenly a gap was made in the wire away to my right. With mad yells of triumph the Druses poured through and charged upon the trenches. In the blue glare of the Verey lights we could see their contorted faces, their long glittering swords.

But not one reached the trenches. A couple of machine-guns caught them as they swept through the gap, mowing them down.

Gradually the firing dwindled and at length ceased. We had beaten them off—at any rate, for the time being.

The captain called for volunteers to go out and mend the wire. Every man was eager to go, and ten Russians and a corporal were selected for the task. In silence they crawled out over the top, carrying with them a couple of reels of rusty barbed wire and some iron stakes.

The minutes passed. Then a low choking cry broke the silence. Gripping our rifles, we peered into the darkness, ready to repel another attack.

A few moments later the corporal and five of
the Russians came stumbling back over the
parapet. As they jumped down into the trench
the captain came striding up to know if they had
repaired the gap in the wire.

"*Mon Dieu*, it is impossible," answered the
corporal. "We can do nothing. Five of the men
have had their throats cut already and their
heads are off. The Druses are lying among the
dead bodies out there. It is impossible to tell
the living from the dead. They rise up as we
pass and cut us down with their knives."

It would have been murder to have sent out
more men in an attempt to mend the wire. The
only thing to be done was to wait for the daylight, when it would be possible to distinguish
the living from the dead. In the meantime that
gap in the wire had to be very carefully watched.
If the enemy renewed the attack they would be
certain to concentrate on that point.

Perhaps an hour passed in tense vigilance. All
was silent except for the moans and cries of the
wounded Druses and the clanking and creaking of
the wire as they struggled to free themselves.
Occasionally, far away in the distance, could be
heard the howl of a jackal.

Our losses, so far, were seven killed and six

wounded. The dead were lifted out of the trench, the wounded carried back to the mud huts. There was no medical officer and nothing in the way of a properly-organized dressing-station. A dab of iodine and a rough bandage was the only available treatment. For the rest, one had to rely upon luck and providence.

Fortunately we had an ample supply of Verey lights, and by sending one up every few minutes we were able to keep a keen watch. Every man remained at his post and there was no question of our vigilance being relaxed. The captain, revolver in hand, strode from post to post, making sure that everything was in order.

We were beginning to think that the enemy had abandoned the attack when suddenly there came the thudding of hoofs. As a Verey light burst we saw a hundred or more horsemen sweep out of the darkness and charge, hell for leather, straight at the gap in the wire.

We opened out with rifles and machine-guns. Dozens of horses and riders fell. But nothing could stop that onrushing wave of yelling humanity. They were on top of us, cutting, thrusting, stabbing.

The trench became an inferno of kicking horses and struggling men. In the darkness both sides fought like demons. It was a wild, elemental encounter, with every man for himself. Kill or be killed.

As I rushed along the trench towards the captain a tall, white-robed figure loomed out of the darkness. I could hear the sweep of his sword. But instinctively I shot him at point-blank range and he sank with a thud at my feet. Another wounded Druse stabbed at me from the parapet as I passed. I plunged my bayonet into him with such force that I was unable to withdraw it. Then, sabre in hand, I went on to join the captain.

He was in the centre of a group of struggling, dimly seen forms. I could hear his voice screaming above the din. Then, as a Verey light burst, I saw his great cavalry sabre swinging and a Druse crumple up before it. An instant later he had plunged it through the throat of another. I shot two more of his opponents with my revolver.

Then the end came abruptly. The few remaining survivors of the charge crept away into the darkness. We had beaten them off again.

Our first task was to clear the trenches. They were a welter of mud and blood. Dead, dying, and wounded, men and horses, lay in heaps. The dead were flung out over the parapet. Our own wounded were carried back to the camp. The wounded Druses were killed with a sabre thrust and flung over the top. It was brutal, but it was the captain's order. "Finish the swine off!" he said. After all, there was nothing else we could do, for we had no real accommodation for our own wounded. In any case, it put them out of their misery.

The murderous work was carried out in silence. All the time our senses were alert, for at any moment the enemy might renew the attack.

They remained quiet, however, although we could occasionally hear them in the darkness carrying off their wounded who were lying on the farther side of the wire.

At last the night of horror came to an end and the dawn broke. The sun rose over the distant horizon, filling the desert with its joyous beams.

The enemy had disappeared, but a hideous scene remained. The trenches were reeking with blood. The parapet, the wire and beyond were littered with the dead.

Within a few moments everybody, from the captain downwards, was over the top and busy looting the bodies.

All I managed to find were a couple of silver medjidies, worth about fifty francs. The captain was luckier, his booty including fifty gold medjidies, a silk scarf, and a number of knives and revolvers. The lieutenant found a beautiful curved sword of Damascus steel with a gold hilt. Several found gold lockets and chains and the models of the sacred Golden Calf which the Druses wear as talismans.

The looting over, the dead Druses were tied together in grisly bundles and dragged out into the desert where they were left for the jackals and hyenas to fight over. Within a week there were only a few bones left to bleach in the sun.

Our own dead were buried.

By the time that the last body had been hauled out into the wilderness reaction was beginning to set in after the strain of the night. Men were staggering and stumbling as they lurched along. When they spoke it was to snarl a curse at their neighbours. But there was still work to be done. The trenches had to be cleaned and repaired, the wire mended, the wounded tended.

As the captain's batman, I missed these duties and was free to go back to my hut. Flinging myself down, I lay staring at the mud walls. I was quivering in every limb and cold beads of sweat were trickling down my face. It was the reaction. I pictured myself lying dead out there in the desert, waiting for the jackals. I thought of the men I had killed, of the hideous business of slaughtering the wounded. In vain I tried to thrust the thoughts away from me ; the memories seemed more vivid and more ghastly than the actual events. The desire filled me to run away, to dash blindly across the desert, away from all this horror.

The facts that I had come through the battle without a scratch, that we had won a victory, counted for nothing. Never have I felt so utterly and completely miserable. I just wanted to weep and keep on weeping.

Every soldier, I suppose, knows those "after the battle" blues. It is Nature balancing her accounts. Before the fight there is that period of nervous tension. During it, there is all the wild excitement and fierce exultation. Afterwards, one just drops into a pit of depression. Victory always seems rotten to the men who win it. They leave the cheering and the joy bells to those who stay at home.

After a time I stripped and washed and did what I could to remove the dirt and grime from my clothes. I felt better after that and went along to help look after the wounded.

With all the dirt of battle and their blood

caked upon them, these poor devils were lying in hell. Even if the medical corporal had known anything about his job, he would have been utterly helpless for lack of supplies. The most that we could do was to wash them, bandage their wounds, and give them drinks of wine and water.

Some had fallen into unconsciousness and were hovering between life and death. Some were delirious and screaming wildly. Some were cursing and blaspheming, filling the air with obscenity. Some were joking.

I found the Swiss boy who had been my companion on guard on the night of my arrival. He had been shot through the chest and was spitting blood every few moments. He was taking no notice of his surroundings and was weeping quietly to himself. Perhaps he was thinking of his native village far away in the Alps, of the tragic ruin circumstance had made of his young life. I did my best to cheer him up, telling him that the supply train would arrive soon and that in a few hours he would be safe in the hospital at Damascus. But he did not seem to be listening to me.

Occasionally his lips moved. I think he was praying.

And that was the first and only time during my

period in the Legion that I saw a man admit that
religion meant anything to him at all.

I doubt if he was twenty—a mere boy for whom
life should have been a thing of joyous sunshine
and brave ideals. Of course, he had been a fool—
he had stolen money and squandered it on a
worthless siren of a circus girl. But was his sin
so great that he deserved to be smashed in the
hideous business of war ?

He was praying as he lay there on the brink
of death. Perhaps in spite of everything he still
found it possible to believe in a God who could be
merciful.

It was towards midday when that long-delayed
supply train arrived.

The captain, not in the best of moods, strode
along and angrily demanded to know why his
urgent messages had been ignored.

The commandant of the train blandly explained
that the train could have reached us days before,
but in view of the fact that we were about to be
attacked it had been decided to wait until we had
beaten off the enemy.

I thought for a moment that the captain was
going to knock him down.

"The devil you did !" he roared. "Do you know
that we haven't enough ammunition left to fill

a machine-gun belt ? Do you know that for the past two days we've been on half rations ? Do you know that if the enemy had made another attack there would not have been one of us left alive ? And you considered it prudent to wait until it was quite safe before you came to our aid ! For weeks I've been clamouring for those supplies! But a few hours' extra delay meant nothing to you so long as your own precious skin was safe ! We could be all murdered, but you and your wretched train must not run into danger ! *Mon Dieu*, this shall be reported to the general ! "

Later, the captain did lodge a complaint, but so far as I am aware nothing ever came of it. The incident was typical of the casual way in which the Legion was treated by the rest of the Army. We were merely the blackguards who had to do the dirty work. It really did not matter whether we were wiped out or not ; there were many more blackguards to take our places. It certainly was not worth risking good lives in order to keep us supplied with ammunition.

It was something, however, that the train did actually arrive. In addition to fresh supplies of ammunition it brought stocks of rations, including two barrels of rum and two of wine.

Our wounded were taken off by the train. These

poor wretches had been suffering agonies under the wholly incompetent ministrations of the so-called medical corporal and his amateur helpers. Many of them had died since the morning ; many more doubtless died during the long, jolting journey across the desert ; but the survivors who reached Damascus presumably found some sort of hospital and a real doctor.

I was not the only one who came to the conclusion that it was preferable to be killed outright than to be wounded whilst serving with the Legion in Syria. There was no question of praying for a comfortable "Blighty one" as we did in the old days.

Some time after the train had steamed away in the direction of Damascus a party of Bedouin head-hunters rode up to the camp and announced that they were going to take up a position among the rocks with a view to ambushing any Druses who might return under cover of darkness for the purpose of carrying off their dead. They accordingly asked us to be careful not to fire in the direction of the rocks.

Of course, it might be that they really did spend the night waiting for the Druses. On the other hand, it was possible that they were busy removing the heads from the bodies which we had dragged out into the desert. These, at a hundred francs apiece, represented very easy money for the head-hunters. In any case, there was no sign of the Druses returning during the night, and in the morning the Bedouins had departed.

And they did not return to offer us a commission on the very handsome profit they made out of our battle!

The next few days were more than strenuous. There was much to be done; the trenches had to be repaired and the wire strengthened; stores had to be sorted and stacked. We had lost over a hundred men in the attack and there were only eighty of us left. In addition to the work, of course, there was the necessity of maintaining a constant vigilance in case the enemy should attack again.

The captain worked as hard as any of us, and he saw to it that the N.C.O.s did the same. That was the secret of his greatness as an officer. Whenever there was hard fighting or work to be done he was always ready to do his full share. He was not one of those officers who think that their sole duty is to give orders. He was one of us, as well as our leader.

Then at last the great news arrived that we were to be relieved at Mesmie and were to go "on rest".

Nobody knew where our resting-place was to be, but it was not long before the most enthusiastic rumours were in circulation. We were bound for a legionnaire's paradise, where there was wine in plenty and the population consisted chiefly of beautiful girls unhampered by morals.

One thing was certain. Wherever we went it could not be worse than the dreary desert outpost of Mesmie.

CHAPTER VII

RAYEK, REST, AND ROMANCE

IN due course we were relieved at Mesmie by a battalion of Senegalese. They were 500 strong —quite a crowd in comparison with our depleted numbers. Most of them were black, but a large proportion, possibly a hundred or so, were Frenchmen.

These, I learnt, were murderers, thieves, apaches, forgers, and various other sorts of criminals. They looked it, and some of the legionnaires would almost have passed as gentlemen in comparison with them.

When a Frenchman, I gather, commits a serious crime before reaching military age, he is drafted, on being called up, to one of the colonial battalions. Moreover, after doing their eighteen months' service they are given a bonus of 6,000 francs if they sign on for a further five years. At least, that is what I was told.

At first I was very indignant at the idea of white

men being forced to serve in the ranks with blacks. After I had seen a little more of the whites I felt sorry for the blacks, most of whom were little more than boys.

After bidding Mesmie an enthusiastic farewell we indulged in the usual interminable railway journey over badly-laid track in springless cattle-trucks. Owing to our losses, however, we had comparatively plenty of room.

Our holiday home turned out to be the charming little Arab town of Rayek—at any rate, it seemed charming after Mesmie. It was peaceful, far from the Djebel Druses; it contained cafés where *vin rouge* could be obtained in plenty; and the population included a certain number of ladies of various descriptions. What more could legionnaires require? Rayek was a home from home.

Of course, it was not all play and no work. There was the usual drill without which no army "rest" is complete, and there was the inevitable musketry. Moreover, a few days after our arrival, a consignment of wild Arab horses turned up and we were given the task of breaking them in.

It was an exciting job, for those horses were utterly untamed, and at the mere sight of a man their ears went back ominously. They kicked and bit with equal facility. The order to mount was

130

always followed by a wild-west rodeo exhibition, with the horses rearing, biting, kicking, and rolling. There were several broken arms and legs and other injuries before we succeeded in bringing those beasts to a reasonable frame of mind. The only people who really enjoyed it were the Cossacks. They were used to it. The Germans and Swiss hated it.

I did not exactly revel in the task myself, my experience of horses, previous to my joining the Legion, having been confined to pit ponies. But by a stroke of good fortune I succeeded as often as not in dodging the rodeo. The local commandant was very keen on learning English, and as I was the only Englishman available, he selected me as his teacher. It was not perhaps an ideal arrangement, from the educational point of view, for my knowledge of French could only be described as scrappy, and I do not claim to be a master of English. But the commandant was satisfied—and so was I. It was much pleasanter to try to teach him English than to have my neck broken by a wild Arab steed.

In the evenings we were more or less free to do as we liked. The result, of course, was that there were a good many wild nights with trouble to follow. The commandant was very worried about

131

it and was all for stern discipline. We had, however, a good friend in our captain. He knew what we had been through at Mesmie and he considered that we deserved a holiday. Many a man who in ordinary circumstances would have found himself in the cells escaped scot-free, thanks to him. He often joined us in a café and stood drinks all round, swapping yarns with the rest of us as if he were one of ourselves.

The pedantic disciplinarian would have been horrified, but as a matter of fact it was the wisest thing he could have done. We were a rough, calloused crowd, little better than brutes, but he won such loyalty and affection as was left to us. We realized that we had a pal as well as an officer, and we were ready to follow him through hell itself.

God knows he had his faults. There were times when he was little better than a maniac. But he had the secret of commanding men. He may not have shown up well on the parade ground, with its "spit and polish", but in action he was worth a dozen barrack-square martinets.

The idea that an officer is a superior class of being who must never come off his pedestal, may have been all right years ago, but it doesn't carry much weight in these democratic days. Still less

does it succeed with a "tough" crowd like the
Legion, where there is no fear either of God or
of man. We could be lashed into sulky submission,
but the better way was to win our trust. We knew
that he could be relied upon always to play the
game.

It is officers such as he who win wars.

One evening Georgia, another Russian called
Bedakov, and I, were sitting in an Arab café
yarning about things in general over a bottle
of wine when suddenly we heard a woman
screaming in the room above us.

"That's Russian !" exclaimed Bedakov, jumping
to his feet. And before we could stop him he was
dashing up the stairs three at a time.

"Come back, you fool !" I shouted. "You'll
only get into trouble !"

Bedakov, however, had already disappeared
from sight. The next thing we heard was the crash
of a door being burst off its hinges. It was followed
by a lot of swearing in Russian and Arabic and
the sound of a struggle. The screaming ceased.

Downstairs in the café—we were the only
Europeans present—there was pandemonium.
Everybody was shouting at once.

"Come on," I said to Georgia. "We'd better
go and see what's happening !"

Drawing our revolvers, we forced our way through the crowd and rushed up the stairs.

Two Arabs, considerably the worse for wear, were lying on the floor. Bedakov was standing over them, his revolver in his hand. A girl, sobbing and terrified, was cowering in a corner.

"What the devil do you think you're doing?" demanded Georgia, going over to Bedakov. "You ought to know better than to interfere with the natives! There'll be a hell of a row about this, and we shall all get it in the neck!"

Bedakov nodded in the direction of the girl. "She's Russian," he said.

It was then that we saw that the girl, in spite of her oriental costume, was European. She was remarkably pretty, too.

By this time the room was becoming crowded with jabbering Arabs. The proprietor of the café was particularly loud in his protestations.

The first thing we did was to clear the Arabs out of the room. Some of them were inclined to fight and attempt to rescue their damaged compatriots. Our revolvers, however, cowed them and, aided by a few kicks, they trooped back down the stairs, all talking at the tops of their voices. The proprietor was quietened by the promise that he should be paid for all damage done and by the threat that, if he was not careful, he would be reported to the authorities.

Meanwhile Bedakov was still standing over the two cowering Arabs, who appeared to be of the merchant class. Their eyes were fixed on the muzzle of his revolver. The girl was still crouching in the corner, trembling and sobbing.

"Look after these two swine, will you?" said Bedakov to us when we had cleared the room. He then went over to the girl and picked her up in his arms.

For some time she was unable to do more than sob and cling to him, but after a while he managed to get her story from her.

She was the daughter of a Russian refugee who had settled in Beyrout. There she had met one of the Arabs who had posed as a great chief and had made violent love to her. Fascinated by the imitation sheik, the girl had at last agreed to go away with him.

Soon the glamour of romance had disappeared. The sheik lover had grown tired of his white bride, and within less than a month she had found herself in the position of a slave, beaten and subjected to every indignity. Finally he had brought her to the café and had sold her to the other Arab for 500 francs. The screams which had brought Bedakov on the scene had been caused by her new owner's attempts to tear her clothes off her after she had refused to strip.

"Oh, that's it, is it ?" said Bedakov, striding over to the two prostrate Arabs. "You couple of——"

When Bedakov had exhausted his vocabulary we had a discussion as to what was to be done. Bedakov was for thrashing the two scoundrels to within an inch of their lives. But Georgia pointed out that it would be advisable to avoid trouble as much as possible. We accordingly contented ourselves with taking the 500 francs which the imitation sheik had been paid. After handing the money over to the girl, we called the proprietor of the café and asked him how much he wanted for the damage done to his premises. With a wealth of eloquence he protested that 200 francs would make but small amends for all that he had suffered.

"Pay him 200 francs," ordered Bedakov, stirring the two Arabs with a kick.

There was the usual eloquence about their being poor men, to whom such a sum was wealth beyond their fondest dreams.

"Pay !" said Bedakov, fingering the butt of his revolver.

They paid.

"And now," said Bedakov, "you can go. And if I see your ugly faces in Rayek again I'll——"

But the Arabs did not wait to hear what would happen. They scrambled to their feet and darted from the room.

We took the girl along to a Frenchwoman and left her in her charge, Bedakov making her promise not to venture out until he came to see her again. She nodded, her large dark eyes gleaming with gratitude.

Georgia and I glanced at each other. It was obviously a case with Bedakov, and the girl evidently regarded him as a sort of knight-errant hero belonging to the realms of chivalry and romance. In the circumstances, Georgia and I were distinctly *de trop*. We accordingly slipped quietly away and left the two of them gazing into each other's eyes.

"Isn't Natalie wonderful?" exclaimed Bedakov when he rejoined us an hour or two later. "Did ever you see such a beautiful girl?"

She was certainly very pretty, though hardly perhaps deserving such extravagant praise. As we did not want a fight, however, Georgia and I agreed that she was wonderful.

Bedakov was very dreamy the next day and as early as possible he slipped away to see Natalie.

"It's all arranged," he confided to us when he returned late in the evening. "I'm going to escape from the Legion and we're getting married just as soon as we can."

"Are you in love with her?" asked Georgia.

"Of course I'm in love with her. And she's in love with me! We're crazy about each other!"

Their plan had the merit of simplicity. Natalie was obtaining a set of civilian clothes for Bedakov —fortunately he was not an out-size—and buying a couple of railway tickets for Beyrout. There was a train leaving in the evening which would give the lovers a start of at least twelve hours. Once in Beyrout, Natalie was sure that her father would give them every assistance.

The plan was a complete success. Georgia and I wished Bedakov the best of luck and the next we heard of him was a letter from South America which reached us three months later. Natalie's father had not only given the happy couple his blessing but the means of making a fresh start in the New World. Bedakov assured us that he and his wife were still as much in love with each other as ever, and he enclosed a note for 1,000 francs with a request that we should drink their healths.

Needless to say, that request was duly complied with.

Who knows ? Perhaps they are still a pair of happy lovers somewhere in South America. Love, as Georgia remarked to me, is a queer business.

Our rest at Rayek was interrupted by our being ordered to take part in a punitive expedition. Bandits had become particularly active in a certain neighbourhood through which the railway passed, and the chiefs of the local villages had failed either to put a stop to the bandits or to protect· the railway. In fact, there was more than a suspicion that the apparently peaceful villagers were actually the bandits who were causing all the trouble.

It had accordingly been decided to send a battery of "75's" to shell the villages concerned. We were to accompany the artillery as a guard. It was not expected that we should be away from Rayek for more than two or three days.

We set off before dawn, and after a sweltering ride across the desert we arrived at the ruined temple of Baal Bek early in the afternoon. Here we camped beside the railway line whilst the artillery made their preparations for blowing the village to bits.

There was no question of our being attacked and the villagers had departed from their homes.

Having nothing in particular to do and knowing that we should not move on again until the next morning, Georgia, another Russian called Stanchinko, and I, decided to go and explore the ruined temple.

It must have been a splendid building ages ago when, I believe, it was one of the chief temples of the sun god. But all that remained were a few broken columns and several heaps of tumbled masonry. Most of it lies buried in the sand.

We had wandered about for some time and were discussing the advisability of getting back to camp in case the artillery dropped a few shells on the temple as well as on the village, when suddenly a venerable Arab appeared from behind a pillar. He had a long white beard and was the oldest man I have ever seen. He must have been at least a hundred years old.

But the amazing thing was that we could have sworn that he had not been behind that pillar five minutes before. And it was impossible for him to have approached that pillar without our noticing him.

He seemed equally surprised at seeing us.

"Hullo ! Who are you ?" we demanded, gripping our revolvers.

"I am the guardian of the temple," he answered. "There are no priests of the sun god left. Only I, the guardian of this holy ground, remain."

"Where do you live ? In the village ?"

"The temple is my home."

"How did you get behind that pillar ?"

He shrugged his shoulders.

"The fact is," remarked Georgia, "he has some sort of a secret hiding-place underground and the entrance is behind that column."

"And it's a hundred to one," added Stanchinko optimistically, "that he has a lot of treasure hidden away too ! Gold, and diamonds, and rubies, and all that sort of thing !"

This seemed an inviting possibility. What was more likely than that the ancient priests should have collected a secret hoard of treasure ? We had all read and heard of such things.

"Why not make him show us round ?" I suggested. "Perhaps we'll be able to spot something."

Meanwhile the old Arab, unable to understand what we were saying, was regarding us with a solemn impassivity.

He did not take kindly to the suggestion that he should show us over his secret underground

141

home, protesting that we were infidel dogs and that our presence was a desecration.

Our revolvers, however, proved a persuasive argument, and after a time he agreed on condition that we swore not to reveal his secret to anybody and made a suitable offering to his master, the sun god. We swore to keep anything we might see strictly to ourselves and gave him ten francs as our offering to the sun god.

Everybody being satisfied, we set off.

"Don't forget!" I warned him, putting my revolver under his nose. "If you try any tricks, you won't have time to be sorry!"

Going round behind the column, he thrust his arm down a small hole and released a catch. This enabled him to move a great hinged slab, revealing a flight of steps below.

"Enter, my friends," said the Arab.

"Think it's all right?" asked Georgia, gazing dubiously at the hole.

"Let's risk it!" said Stanchinko whose mind was full of diamonds and rubies. "We'll keep an eye on the old blighter!"

Georgia went first. The old man followed with Stanchinko and I close at his heels and our revolvers pressing against his ribs.

A torch was produced, and whilst Georgia was

lighting this we helped the old man close the stone slab, at the same time taking care to see how to open it again.

We then proceeded along the passage. The atmosphere was stale and stifling, and the smoke from the torch did not improve matters.

The passage came to a sudden stop in a wall of stone, but our guide opened another secret door in the side. This led us to a great hall.

It looked immense in the lurid, flickering light of the torch and there was something eerie in the silence. The air was clearer than in the passages but it had a curious musty smell, something like incense. It was like being in a huge tomb.

The further end of the hall was completely covered by a curtain stretching from wall to wall.

"What's on the other side of that ?" I asked.

"That is the home of the sun god," he answered. "Only his priest may venture beyond that curtain. If you, an infidel dog, should dare to defile the holy of holies with your presence, the might of the great god would strike you dead."

Perhaps it was the eerie surroundings ; perhaps it was the utter simplicity of his tone. In any case, I almost believed him.

"Where do you live ?" I asked.

"Yonder is my home," he answered, pointing to a door.

Passing through the door, we found ourselves in a small apartment. The floor was carpeted and the walls were hung with curtains. Everything was obviously of extreme antiquity.

"How long have you been here ?" I asked.

"All my life," answered the old man. "For centuries my family has been the guardian of the holy temple. When I am dead my son will be the guardian."

I was on the point of asking him whether his wife and family lived in the village or were prisoners under the ruined temple, when Stanchinko pulled back the carpet and revealed a great iron ring in the centre of a stone slab.

It was obviously the entrance to another secret passage.

The old Arab's manner changed as if by magic. His solemn dignity vanished and he began to quake and tremble.

"Where does that lead to ?" we demanded.

"It is nothing ! Nothing !" protested the Arab, fumbling agitatedly at his beard.

We glanced at each other. This was the entrance to the secret treasure house ! Beneath our feet was all the fabulous wealth of the East.

The old man became frantic in his protests, but three revolvers soon reduced him to a state of incoherent terror.

Seizing the iron ring, we soon shifted the stone slab. Then forcing the old man to lead the way, we scrambled down the steps below.

"Show us where it's hidden!" I ordered, pressing my revolver against his ear. "And don't waste any time!"

Moaning and muttering, he led the way along the passage. Stanchinko was chuckling hysterically. He could already feel his pockets bulging with diamonds and rubies.

At last we reached a door. With a despairing groan the guardian of the temple flung it open. Beyond was a large rectangular cellar.

It contained no gold, or diamonds, or rubies.

But there were stacks of up-to-date rifles and boxes of ammunition.

In the flickering light of the torch we stared at the rifles and then at each other. The old Arab was on his knees, reminding us that we had sworn to reveal nothing.

"Let's get out of this!" said Stanchinko disgustedly.

The last we saw of that Arab he was still

imploring us to remember that we had sworn to keep his secret to ourselves.

As we made our way back to the camp the guns were busy pounding the defenceless village and filling the air with smoke and dust.

After some discussion we decided to say nothing about our adventure. Stanchinko's optimism recovered quickly from the shock, and it occurred to him that there might be treasure hidden away under the temple as well as rifles and ammunition. As he said, it might be well worth while to return some day and investigate matters for ourselves.

The opportunity for this enterprise, however, never came our way, and for all I know the treasure of Stanchinko's dreams is still lying hidden beneath the ruined temple of Baal Bek.

One thing is certain : Stanchinko will never know the truth of his theory. Within a few hours of our adventure in the temple a Druse bullet brought his optimism to a sudden conclusion.

The artillery had duly completed its target-practice and blown the mud huts of some half-dozen villages to smithereens when the news came that a large force of the enemy were concentrating in the ruins of a village three or four miles away.

There was an immediate difference of opinion as to what should be done. Our captain was all for attacking at once. The artillery commander, on the other hand, was of a more cautious disposition. He pointed out that we did not know how strong the enemy were and how serious the consequences might be if his guns fell into the hands of the Druses, who had no artillery of their own. He considered that it would be more prudent to withdraw to Rayek as quickly as possible and report matters to the general. The captain protested that he had never run away in his life and was not going to start now.

Ultimately a compromise was arranged. The artillery commander realized that if we attacked the Druses he and his guns would at any rate obtain a safe start. So the Legion went forward to the attack whilst the artillery—who could have blown the enemy to bits from a safe distance—packed up and made for Rayek by the quickest and shortest route.

As usual, the Legion was being left to do the dirty work !

With our scouts ahead, we cantered forward. It was not long before we heard the sound of firing and the bullets began to whizz. Extending over a wide front, we continued our advance at a steady pace, saving our horses as much as possible.

When we came within sight of the village, or

147

what the guns had left of it, the firing began in earnest. Bullets whirred and whistled past us. Splashes of sand flecked the desert. A man fell here ; a horse there.

The captain might have given the order to dismount. The horses could have been removed to safety and we could have dug ourselves in, returning the enemy's fire. But the skipper had the Cavalryman's dislike for Infantry methods. Besides, we had no fresh supplies of ammunition to fall back upon. It was a case of get on or get out.

There was no doubt as to which course the captain would choose. The fact that he did not know how many of the enemy were lying concealed in the ruined village was a mere detail. Digging his spurs into his horse, he dashed forward, waving his sword and uttering that bloodthirsty yell which would have made the hair of Satan himself stand on end.

There was no need for him to look back to see if we were following him. With a fierce shout the whole line swept forward in a cloud of dust.

For a moment the enemy seemed to waver and the firing slackened. Then they began to pump bullets into us for all they were worth.

Men and horses were falling on right and left.

Before me, a dim figure through the dust thrown

up by his horse's hoofs, I could see the captain. I could hear him yelling at the top of his voice. A bullet flicked against the blade of my sabre.

We were upon them in a thunder of hoofs. Hacking, slashing, riding them down. Nothing could stop us.

They broke and fled, making for the rocky ground beyond the village. But few reached it. We charged through them again and again, cutting them down. Some of them, realizing that escape was impossible, turned and fought to the last.

It was all over in a few minutes. We drew rein, breathless, sweating, and the blood dripping from our sabres.

"Hullo, Harvey !" shouted the captain, clapping me on the back. "Have you got any cigarettes ?"

There was no question of a counter-attack. The remnants of the enemy were in full flight towards the hills.

Our losses were nine killed and twenty-two wounded.

The dead were buried ; the wounded collected and given such first-aid treatment as was possible in the circumstances. Then, having nothing further to do, we set off on the return journey.

We were almost within sight of Rayek when we

encountered the advance guard of the battalion of
Infantry which was being sent to our assistance.

The next day we were paraded before the general,
who made a long and complimentary speech and
gave decorations to some of the wounded.

I don't know whether the artillery commander
received anything, but our captain did not get a
medal. The authorities, of course, regarded him
as a hopeless eccentric who ought not to be
encouraged.

I don't think it worried him ; and it certainly
did not worry us. We were too anxious to resume
our interrupted holiday at Rayek.

It was shortly after this that Klaus disappeared
from the Legion.

He was a wiry, rat-faced little man who had
already spent nearly a year in Syria without
getting a scratch, a feat which made him the
doyen of the squadron. He was a good man in a
fight and did not know the meaning of fear, but
he was an inveterate thief. Stealing was second
nature with him and he was incapable of keeping
his fingers off other people's property. He robbed
his comrades, the sergeants, and even the officers.
He was clever, too, and it was rarely that he was
caught and received the thrashing he deserved.

It was rather a relief to the rest of us when

Klaus met a Syrian girl in the town and fell in love with her. It was too much to expect that love would reform him, but at any rate it provided him with some other occupation than rifling our belongings when we were not looking.

Klaus took his romance very seriously and developed into a most devoted lover, spending all his spare time in the Syrian damsel's company. What attraction he found in her was a mystery to the rest of us, for she could not be described as a Venus. She was plain, even for a Syrian girl. On the other hand, there was no danger of Klaus being mistaken for a matinée idol, so they were all square on that point.

In any case, the two of them appeared to have got it very badly, and the girl used to hang around our quarters in the hope of seeing her hero. As Georgia remarked, love was a funny thing.

Then came the morning when it was discovered that Klaus was missing.

Four rifles had disappeared also from the stores and, what was much more important from our point of view, most of our hard-earned cash had vanished. Of course, the Syrian girl was missing.

The loss of our money stung us to eloquent indignation, and for the first and only time in my experience a man escaped from the Legion without the good wishes of his comrades. Indeed, nobody was more anxious for the recapture of the deserter than we were.

A hue and cry was raised by the authorities ; trains were searched ; innumerable questions asked. But no more was seen of Klaus—or the missing rifles—or our money.

It was ultimately decided that the Syrian girl must have provided him with an Arab disguise and that they must have ridden off together to the hills. Soon the whole of Syria was on the look-out for a fugitive legionnaire disguised as an Arab.

The next act in the romance, although nobody associated Klaus with it at the time, was the attack on a train by some Syrian bandits. These attacks, of course, were an everyday feature of Syrian railway travel, but there were special characteristics in this outrage which marked it off as different from the rest. It was not the ordinary spectacular but comparatively harmless affair of a few pot-shots at a passing train. It had been organized with a business-like efficiency. The lines had been torn up, the train derailed, and the passengers pillaged with a thoroughness worthy of the Wild West. The bandits, evidently, were beginning to learn their business.

Then, a week or so later, Klaus returned, unkempt, ragged, wounded, a prisoner and hand-cuffed.

Klaus had always taken an interest in the activities of the bandits, and had long since come to the conclusion that there was money to be made in the business if it were run on up-to-date lines. The bandits needed organizing and training. They needed a real leader. In short, they needed Klaus.

These ideas had been maturing in his mind for some time, when he met the Syrian girl and discovered that she was the granddaughter of the chief of a gang of bandits whose headquarters were away in the hills.

Klaus's ideas had soon developed. Why not desert from the Legion, elope with the girl to the hills, show her grandfather how to carry on the bandit business, supplant him in the leadership of the gang, and make a fortune ?

It seemed good to Klaus, and his Syrian damsel, who was immensely proud of having a white lover, was only too glad to assist him. She had obtained a burnous for him, generally made the arrangements for his escape, and duly took him off to the hills and introduced him to her grandfather.

The old man received him politely, listened to his views on the art of holding-up trains, and agreed to his giving a practical demonstration of how it should be done. The demonstration had been a great success, and Klaus had become more and more confident that he had at last found his true *métier*. He could see himself becoming the Terror of Syria and ultimately retiring with a huge fortune.

On the return of the gang to the hills, however, a rude shock awaited him. The old chief had not only appropriated all the booty but had denounced Klaus as a French spy. Probably he had guessed that it was the new recruit's ambition to supplant him in the leadership.

There had been a fight and Klaus had succeeded in getting away with a bullet through his shoulder. After wandering for days and nights among the hills and suffering terribly from hunger and thirst, to say nothing of the sweltering heat, he had been found by some Arabs who, recognizing him as a deserter from the Legion, had handed him over to the French.

At the court-martial Klaus had put up the plea that he had been actuated solely by the desire to discover the headquarters of the bandits. It was proved, however, that he had taken a leading part in the attack on the train and he was sentenced to be shot.

No tears were shed. But there was still a good deal of bad language when any reference was made to our missing cash.

There was a good deal of discussion, however, on his idea of turning bandit, and many thought that it deserved serious consideration. Klaus's mistake, it was argued, lay in his reliance upon Arabs as his rank and file.

Now if the whole squadron was to desert and form a real first-class gang of bandits run on co-operative lines——!

For weeks this tantalizing suggestion was discussed. Of course it came to nothing, but it amused us to think and talk of the wonderful things we would do—when we raised the Jolly Roger in the Syrian desert.

We might even capture and sack Damascus!

CHAPTER VIII

COLLECTING THE TAXES

D RAFTS from Sousse had brought us up to full strength again and in due course our rest at Rayek came to an end. We received orders to proceed to the fortress of Rashaya, away up in the hills of the Grand Lebanon country. On our way we were to assist in the collection of taxes.

So far as I could observe, collecting the taxes is the one thing that matters in the French colonial administration. Indeed, the official view appeared to be that the natives existed solely for the purpose of paying for the doubtful blessing of living under the Tricolour. I could never discover that the natives received anything in return for their payments.

Apparently, the inhabitants of some of the villages had come to the same conclusion and were refusing to pay. Hence our orders to assist the collectors.

We rode out of Rayek at four o'clock one morning and by dawn we were well up in the mountains. It was a dreary journey through arid, rocky country, broken here and there by a pitiful little patch of maize cultivated by some industrious Bedouin.

An aeroplane accompanied us for the purpose of conveying the money to Damascus as soon as we had collected it. The authorities apparently were not going to leave it in our keeping any longer than they could help.

At last we reached the village of Tel-y-Ded, where the taxes were in arrear. It was a dismal-looking collection of mud and reed huts surrounded by parched fields where horses, goats, and sheep browsed.

The inhabitants, it must be remembered, had nothing to do with the Djebel Druses, who were definitely at war with France. They were Christian Arabs supposed to be living under the protecting mandate of France. They were our friends.

Having surrounded the village, the captain, with a bodyguard in which I was included, rode into the collection of huts. The aeroplane, flying low, circled over our heads.

We were received by the head man, a fine-looking old fellow with flowing white robes. It was then discovered that he could not speak French and that we had no interpreter with us. We accordingly withdrew and the aeroplane was sent to Damascus to repair the omission.

When at length the interpreter arrived we returned to the village. The head man was told that if the taxes were not paid within twenty-four hours the village would be burnt. We then encamped for the night, sentries being posted around the village to prevent anybody leaving.

The next day, on the expiry of the twenty-four hours, we returned to the village and again interviewed the head man. But we got no taxes. "My people refuse to pay," the head man told the captain. "They ask what good has France done for them and why should they pay taxes for which they receive nothing in return."

The captain lost his temper and made the most blood-curdling threats. But they had no effect upon the old chief. He just shrugged his shoulders and repeated : "My people refuse to pay."

We withdrew from the village and the airman was sent back to Damascus to report what had happened and to ask for orders.

Meanwhile the village was closely surrounded and nobody was allowed to leave it.

It was late in the afternoon when the airman returned and gave the captain his orders. The village was to be burnt and pillaged.

I naturally expected that the head man would be given a last chance to pay the taxes. But that was not the French way.

While the captain was still reading his orders the airman returned to his machine and took off again. Several times he circled over the village, flying low. The inhabitants, men, women, and children, came pouring out of the huts to stare up at him. Then, swooping upwards, he dropped the first bomb.

A terrific roar, a quiver of the earth, and a sheet of flame and smoke shot up from the far end of the village.

Bomb after bomb was dropped on the defenceless collection of mud and reed huts. Fire broke out in a dozen places and a great pall of smoke hung over the village. The shrieks of the trapped inhabitants made hideous the gathering darkness. Some attempted to escape into the hills ; they were shot down as they ran. The remaining survivors crouched among the smouldering ruins of their homes.

Then at last the aeroplane roared away to the

west ; the silent darkness of the night descended on the scene.

There was no sleep that night ; every man was alert at his post. We knew that the survivors would make a desperate attempt under cover of the darkness to cut a way through the cordon and escape into the hills.

Hours passed. Then suddenly, away on the right, there was a flash and the report of a riffle. It was followed by the sharp *"tat-tat-tat"* of a machine-gun and a burst of firing.

At the first rush the Arabs wiped out a whole machine-gun crew. But that was their only success. They were hopelessly out-numbered and it was easy enough for us to hold them off. They were trapped.

In the grey light of the dawn we were drawn up before the still-smoking ruins and the order was given to charge.

With a thunder of galloping hoofs we swept forward, our sabres glinting in the first rays of the dawn.

The Arabs fired at us with their long muskets from among the ruins of their homes and fought us with sword and knife. Even as they fell under the hoofs of our horses they stabbed at us with the valour of despair. Their women faced the charge as unflinchingly as the men, wielding swords and knives and even farm implements. Many had children clinging to them.

They had not a chance, for they were hopelessly out-numbered. Within a few minutes not one was left alive. Young and old, men, women, and children, all had been massacred.

They were not our enemies. They were peaceful folk, supposed to be living under the protection of France, and their sole crime was the refusal to pay the taxes demanded of them.

During all the time I was with the Legion I saw nothing more brutal or more nauseating than the slaughter of the women and children of Tel-y-Ded.

We looted the smouldering ruins and stripped the dead of their trinkets. Five hundred sheep, two hundred goats, and a dozen horses were sent off to Damascus under escort, in lieu of the unpaid taxes. Some hundreds of chickens which had managed to escape the massacre were eaten in celebration of our "victory".

The authorities had no more trouble with unwilling taxpayers in that neighbourhood.

We had "learnt" them to be Arabs.

CHAPTER IX

RASHAYA

AFTER this exploit we continued on our journey to Rashaya, the mountain fortress which we were to take over and garrison. The road ran along deep, gloom-filled gorges, under beetling cliffs and along the brinks of precipices. The further we advanced the fewer became the signs of human habitation. The people, if ever there had been any in that desolate country, had either been exterminated by the Druses or had escaped to some less turbulent neighbourhood. Occasionally we passed a deserted homestead.

Snipers picked off a couple of men in the advance guard, but otherwise the journey was without incident, and in due course we arrived at Rashaya.

It was a grim, stone-built fortress, standing on a spur of rock. On one side there was a sheer precipice with a torrent at the bottom. On two other sides were the towering mountains, threatening to crash down and sweep away the fortress.

On the fourth side there was the wide military road leading up from the valley, in which were dotted a few Arab huts.

The captain had been remarkably quiet during the journey, but as we rode through the great iron-studded gates he suddenly brightened and started to talk to me in a queer, excited way. I gathered that the squadron had been stationed at Rashaya some months before when a particularly fierce attack had been made by the Druses.

"We gave them hell!" exclaimed the captain, his eyes glittering. "And we'll give them hell again!"

And I noticed how his face was twitching and his hands shaking. He looked ill.

We dismounted in the great courtyard, and the commandant of the troops whom we were relieving started on the formalities of handing over the command of the fortress.

After a time he happened to mention that there were ten Druse prisoners in the cells, awaiting trial.

"Prisoners!" cried the captain, that mad light shining in his eyes. "What do you want prisoners for? Come on, Harvey, we'll soon settle the swine!"

"But you can't kill them!" expostulated the commandant. "They haven't been tried yet!"

"Nonsense!" said the captain. "We'll save the trouble of a trial and the expense of their rations! Come on!"

As his batman and orderly I had no alternative but to follow him. The commandant walked beside him, expostulating all the time.

Two Tirailleurs carrying lighted torches led the way along the dark, damp passages which took us to the cells. At length we halted, and one of them unlocked and opened a ponderous door with a grille in it.

Rats scampered away squeaking as we entered.

By the lurid light of the torches we saw a heap of natives huddled together in a corner of the cell. They looked half-starved and half-dead. The raw red weals of a bull whip could be seen on their backs.

The sight of them filled the captain with a frenzy. Striding over to them, he kicked and lashed the wretches. "Stand up, you swine!" he roared. "Stand up!"

They stood, dazed and shivering, before him. Taking his great Mauser pistol, he deliberately shot them one by one. Then, drawing his sabre, he hacked their bodies, slashing, stabbing and thrusting with a mad ferocity.

In the lurid, flickering light of the torches it was like some hideous nightmare. The commandant's white, scared face—the staring eyeballs of the Tirailleurs—the blue reek of the powder— the quivering bodies—the hot gasping breath of the captain as he stamped and stabbed.

Then at last it was over. The captain was leaning wearily against the wall of the cell, his face ashen grey, his dripping sabre hanging list-lessly in his hand, his uniform soaked with blood. Sweat was pouring down his face. The mad light had vanished from his eyes.

Going over to him, I took him by the arm. "Come on, sir," I said, "you're not well."

Without a word he allowed me to take him back to his headquarters. The commandant followed us, murmuring : *"Mon Dieu !* The man is a demon !"

As soon as we reached his room the captain, bespattered as he was from head to foot with blood, flung himself down on his bed and refused to stir. The business of taking over the fortress had to be attended to by the lieutenant.

The next morning I found the captain tossing and cursing on his bed, raving about Bedouins and prisoners, and crying that his head was going to burst. His uniform, hands and face were still caked with blood.

Realizing that he was ill, I went and fetched the lieutenant. When we returned to the room we found that the captain had staggered across to his sword-belt and was trying to tug his sabre from its scabbard.

"Kill the swine!" he was shouting. "Cut them to pieces! Flog them! Flog them! I'll teach the sons of swine not to pay France!"

I took him by one arm and the lieutenant seized the other. Between us we dragged him, kicking and struggling, back to bed and strapped him down with leather belts. We then sent for the medical corporal.

The latter, hopelessly incompetent, looked at the raving officer, scratched his head, and announced that it was a case of fever. He then departed, leaving me in charge of the madman.

For six days and nights the captain raved and shrieked, groaned and tossed. All this time he was in his blood-soaked clothes, for in his struggles it was impossible to get them off him. Then at last he went to sleep. For hours he lay there, so still that often I thought that he was dead. But when he awakened he looked at me with normal eyes.

"Hullo, Harvey," he said weakly, "you still alive ? I thought you were dead."

The fever had left him. I fed him with goats' milk, rum and beaten eggs, and chicken broth. Thanks to his iron constitution, he pulled round rapidly and within a couple of days was about again.

We were just beginning to settle down to a quiet stay at Rashaya when the news came that the Druses were massing in the mountains and preparing for a big attack. Probably their spies had told them of the massacre of the prisoners and they were intending to revenge them. So far as I could see, all the inhabitants were ready to pass on information to the Druses. It was not surprising in view of the treatment they received from France.

Having made all preparations for the defence of the fortress, the captain sent the lieutenant with two dozen men to reconnoitre the deep gorge which he called the Devil's Gully. This was the most likely direction from which the enemy would make their attack.

Standing on the battlements, I watched them through a pair of binoculars.

Our men were proceeding slowly up the winding path along the bottom of the ravine, when suddenly white puffs of smoke could be seen among the rocks on either side and above them. They were followed by the faint *crack, crack, crack* of far-away rifles.

I saw several horses and riders fall. The rest wheeled and galloped back to the fort, leaving the wounded behind them. It can be imagined what a hideous fate awaited those wounded at the hands of their Druse captors. It was on them that vengeance was taken for the murder of the Druse prisoners in the fortress dungeon.

I had long since decided to keep one round in my revolver for myself in case I should be hit and in danger of falling into the hands of the enemy.

Our men had hardly returned to the fort when the inhabitants of the huts in the valley came running to the gates, many of them with their few precious belongings, calling for admission and screaming : "The Druses are coming ! The Druses are coming !"

We admitted the women and children, but not the men. We could not trust them and they had to shift for themselves. When they found that they were not to be admitted they made off like cats up the rocky slopes of the gorge.

It soon became evident that the enemy were
going to attack at once. White-robed figures
could be seen creeping closer and closer under
cover of the rocks. It was useless to fire upon
them until they came out into the open. We had
not such a stock of ammunition that we could
afford to waste any. Besides, being acquainted
with the ways of the authorities at Damascus,
we knew that we could not rely on receiving any
fresh supplies.

The knowledge that we had not sufficient
ammunition to hold out indefinitely was not our
only worry. With us in the fortress were a number
of black colonial troops, and it was more than
doubtful whether they would prove of any
assistance. I don't know how they were recruited,
but presumably it was by conscription, and in
any case they did not give the impression of being
fighters. Their skins might be black, but their
livers were white. The captain told me bluntly
that if he could have his way he would bundle
the whole lot out of the fortress and carry on the
defence ourselves.

And there were two obvious points of weakness
in the fortress itself. The great wooden gates
were very old. Fortunately, the enemy had no
artillery—a field-gun would have blown the gates

to smithereens in a second—but the woodwork was already riddled with the rifle-fire of previous encounters, and it was obvious that those gates would not withstand any great strain. Another danger-point was the place where the rocky heights practically overhung the walls and the buildings below. It was not difficult to imagine the fanatical warriors gaining an entrance from that direction.

In addition, of course, we had no means of guessing the strength of the enemy. But it was more than probable that we were heavily out-numbered. On the whole, the situation was not encouraging.

As I watched the white-robed figures creeping from rock to rock, I wondered whether my luck would hold or whether I was one of those who were destined to go under. I had come through the battle at Mesmie without a scratch. Could I hope for such good fortune a second time?

And I realized how slender were my chances of completing my term of five years with the Legion. I might scrape through one, two, or even three battles, but it would be merely putting off the inevitable. Sooner or later the time would come when a Druse knife or bullet would do its work and the jackals would be fighting over my bones.

Life seemed very sweet at that moment, even the desperate and hungry existence which had been my lot before I joined the Legion. I remembered my native village with its coal tips and slag heaps.

Why should I throw my life away for France? What quarrel had I with the Druses? I called to mind Bedakov, Houssmann, and the others who had escaped. Why should not I follow their example and be free again?

The idea of escaping had been lurking in my mind ever since the moment when I had realized that the promises made to me before joining had been nothing but lies. It now became a fixed determination.

The minutes crept by, tense with expectancy. Every man was at his post, staring at the stark rocks and hills, waiting for the death orgy to begin. High overhead some vultures could be seen slowly circling against the cloudless sky. There was a strange quiver in the silence. When a man spoke his voice sounded abnormally loud.

The Legion was guarding all the danger-points. The captain had insisted on this, saying that he was not going to trust his life to a black rabble. He had every justification for his remarks, for several of the niggers were already half-paralysed with fear.

With his sword in one hand and a great Mauser pistol in the other, he hurried from post to post. There was that mad glint in his eyes, and in a thick snarling voice he prophesied that the Legion would give the Druses hell. He offered to bet that he would kill more of the swine than any other man in the fortress.

The men laughed and bandied grisly jokes with him. They loved him. He was the greatest fighter of them all.

Still the tense minutes of waiting dragged on.

Then suddenly the enemy, who had been creeping forward among the rocks, opened a terrific rifle-fire, spraying the walls and the fortress with their bullets. At the same moment a company of cavalry came charging down the road towards the gates. Their war-cry could be heard above the din of the rifle-fire.

We mowed them down by dozens, but still they charged on, as if determined to burst the gates off their hinges by flinging their horses against it. Death meant nothing to these fanatics.

Meanwhile, the riflemen among the rocks continued to pour a terrific fire upon the fortress. The air was filled with the whir of bullets, the shriek of a richochet, the sharp *spat spat* as the missiles struck the stones. Several men were hit.

Then a cloud of smoke and the crackle of flames by the gates revealed the enemy's plan. Whilst our attention had been concentrated on the charging cavalry and the hidden marksmen among the rocks, others had crept forward under the shadow of the walls and had lit a bonfire against the wooden gates. They must have had supplies of petrol or oil, for within a few seconds the gates were blazing.

Pulling their horses up on their haunches, the cavalry wheeled and galloped away. Again and again horse or rider fell.

An attempt was made to put out the fire. Buckets of water were passed along the walls from hand to hand, but few reached their destination. Man after man was picked off by the snipers among the rocks and fell to the courtyard below.

A machine-gun, manned by a Senegalese crew, was mounted in the courtyard ready to deal with the invaders should they burst through the gates.

I don't know how many Druses were taking part in the attack, but it seemed like millions. For every one we shot down, two came pressing forward, yelling their battle-cry. Ladders were thrown across from the rocks to the walls, and again and again they obtained a footing on the walls or the roof of a building. Their courage was

174

amazing. Death meant no more to them than to a mob of shrieking demons.

This fanatical courage had its moral effect upon the defenders of the fort. The men of the Legion were firm enough ; to them it was all part of the day's work. But the black troops, most of them under fire for the first time, were very shaky. Already their officers and N.C.O.s were using whips in order to make them carry out their commands. Some of them lay gibbering at their posts, too paralysed to use their rifles. Others were blazing away with a panicky energy—and wasting ammunition.

I noticed our captain glance at them occasionally and curse. Knowing the capabilities of his temper, I would not have been surprised if he had dashed among them and attempted to drive the whole lot out of the fortress.

I was cramming a fresh clip into my rifle when the blazing gates went down in a furnace of flames, sparks and smoke. Instantly a wild mob of yelling Druses surged in like a wave, their bare feet trampling over the red-hot embers, their swords flashing.

A machine-gun had been posted to deal with this possibility, and it needed only the touch of a finger to mow down those Druses as they came pouring through the gateway. But the black gun-crew did not fire a shot. They just turned and bolted.

The machine-gun, not forty yards from the gate, was left for the enemy to seize and turn upon us. It was a critical moment ; that machine-gun might mean the difference between victory and extermination. The enemy were racing towards it.

Suddenly a young French officer dashed forward. He reached the gun with only a few yards to spare. With a shot from his revolver he wrecked the mechanism. The next instant the Druses were upon him, hacking him to pieces.

It was the bravest deed I ever saw. That officer raced to certain death in order to give the rest of us a chance. It was the greatest sacrifice of all.

Meanwhile the Druses were still pouring through the gates. The courtyard became a battlefield. To add to the confusion our horses broke from their lines and, neighing with terror, galloped madly in all directions.

It was the Legion that cleared the courtyard. The black troops were in a state of hopeless panic. They were gathered in cowering, gibbering groups, their officers and N.C.O.s attempting to flog them into fighting.

From the walls and from behind barricades of our own dead, we legionnaires met the invaders with rifle and machine-gun fire, and with bombs. It was practically point-blank range and every shot told. They went down in heaps. Here and there a few managed to reach our men and hand-to-hand fighting took place. But at last we succeeded in clearing the courtyard and no more of the enemy came pressing forward through the gates.

There were hundreds of dead and dying men and horses lying in the yard, and smoke was still rising from the smouldering embers of the gates. Our rifles were hot, our fingers cramped, our faces black with smoke and sweat.

But there was no time for rest, or even to attend to the ever-growing number of wounded. At any moment the attack on the gates might be renewed ; from the hillside the enemy were still pouring a deadly fire upon us.

Orders had just been given for the gateway to be barricaded with sandbags when word came that the enemy had obtained a footing in one of the houses built against the walls. They had flung ladders across from the rocks and, scrambling across, had entered by means of the roof. Every man defending that portion of the wall had been killed.

Calling to those about him to follow, our captain dashed off to tackle the task of driving the intruders out. He was like that. He had the courage of a tiger and he never ordered a man to undertake a task which he was afraid to attempt himself. There was no need for him to glance back to see if any were following. He knew that with him to lead us we would dare the terrors of hell itself.

With two dozen of us at his heels, he charged into the house.

Within a few moments we were fighting desperately, on the stairs, in passages, on landings, on the roof and parapets. It was hand-to-hand, sword-to-sword, and pistol-to-pistol. It was kill or be killed.

The fanatical courage of the Druses was well-matched against the reckless bravery of the Legion. We were no longer men ; we were savage animals struggling, tooth and claw, for supremacy. We knew neither fatigue nor fear. Kill ! Kill ! Kill !—that was the only thing that mattered. Above the din I could hear my own voice, screaming in hoarse exultation as my sabre cleft the skull of a Druse warrior. I laughed as I wrenched my blade free and felt my enemy's life-blood spurt over me. Nearby a corporal, with one arm cut off at the shoulder, was lying yelling obscenities and firing his rifle with one hand. A Druse darted forward and stabbed him with his long knife. An instant later the Druse fell forward over the corporal's body, his head almost severed by my sabre. Laughing, I dashed on.

It was mad, hideous. But it was fighting.

Gradually, step by step, we forced the enemy back, stumbling over the dead and dying. At last, we had what was left of them on the roof.

Then, from our very feet, came the startling *tat-tat-tat-tat* of a machine-gun. Two of our men had brought a light Hotchkiss and thrust it through a skylight. The Druses went down like ninepins. The survivors, taken completely by surprise, leapt madly from the roof and walls on to the rocks below, where they lay crushed, maimed and bleeding until death put an end to their agony.

We had won another respite.

As I turned away, I saw the captain, covered with blood and grime from head to foot, his eyes ablaze, and his dripping sabre in his hand.

"Hullo, Harvey!" he cried, "still alive! Come on and see what's happening!"

Nothing, I believe, would have pleased him better than to find that the enemy had gained a footing in another corner of the fortress and that another hand-to-hand fight was necessary. As we stumbled down the blood-splashed, body-littered stairs he swayed like a drunken man.

Matters, however, had quietened down. The enemy was still sniping from the rocks and causing several casualties. But no further attack had developed.

The work of barricading the gates was being pushed forward. Dead bodies, sandbags, furniture, everything was flung into the breach.

It was being done by the colonial troops, and never have I seen anything so pitiful. Those men were crazy with terror. Their lips were ashen and their eyes rolling. Dozens of them were weeping and sobbing hysterically. Their officers and N.C.O.s were continually lashing them with long-thronged whips.

But there was no time to waste over pity.

We had beaten off the enemy for the time being, but the situation was desperate. We had no means as yet of ascertaining our loss, but from the few of us who remained it was obvious that our casualties must have been heavy. And there was the usual shortage of supplies. Only two boxes of ammunition remained in the store. Not a bomb was left.

To add to our worries, the telephone operator had been unable to get a message through to Damascus.

We collected all the ammunition from the dead and wounded, and this was carefully shared out. A Hotchkiss machine-gun mounted at a sand-bagged door had six hundred rounds of ammunition—and it would fire four hundred and fifty in the first minute! Other machine-guns had two or three belts in reserve, instead of dozens!

If the enemy attacked again in force we would not have a round of ammunition left within five minutes! After that it would be a case of fighting with bayonet and sabre until the last man fell.

Our next task was to pile the dead three deep on the walls as a protection against the snipers. We then did what we could to ease the sufferings of the wounded. There were comparatively few of them, for in that fierce hand-to-hand fighting the majority had been killed outright. We could do little for them and the medical corporal was worse than useless.

Late in the afternoon the telephone operator

succeeded at last in getting a message through to headquarters at Damascus. There was no need to exaggerate the position. If the enemy attacked again before reinforcements and supplies reached us we would be exterminated and—what perhaps was more important to the authorities—the fortress would be lost. The answer came that relief would be dispatched at once.

Meanwhile the enemy were still sniping from the rocks. We answered with an occasional shot, not wishing to advertise the fact that we were short of ammunition. All the time we were wondering anxiously whether the enemy would attack again before nightfall, or wait until the dawn. If the authorities at Damascus sent Cavalry to our aid, and at once, it should reach us some time during the night.

At last the darkness fell.

It was a night of waking terror. No one slept. We lined the walls and, beleagued behind barricades of the dead, lay peering into the darkness with aching eyes. What were the enemy doing ? Would relief reach us in time ? Occasionally the sharp crack of a rifle broke the stillness. Somebody had seen a shadowy shape flitting among the shadows. Or else it had been a case of nerves. We talked in tense whispers.

Then at last we heard the buzz of an aeroplane in the darkness. The machine circled low over the fortress and there was a thud as the message dropped in the courtyard.

I ran forward and took it to the captain.

"Column has started. Battalion of Infantry and squadron of Cavalry on the way."

The captain cursed. What was the use of sending Cavalry hampered by Infantry? It would be twelve hours or more before they reached us. And it was practically certain that the Druses would attack again at dawn.

That message meant that we were doomed. There was nothing we could do, except prepare to fight to the end. There was no question of surrendering ; the Druses did not take prisoners.

But with the coming of the dawn a faint ray of hope returned to us. The aeroplane did not return to Damascus, but remained circling over the fortress.

The airman's instructions, apparently, were to wait and see what happened. If the Druses attacked and we were wiped out he could return and warn the relief column that there was no need for it to proceed.

But there was a hope that the Druses, having a wholesome terror of being bombed from the air, would think that the aeroplane was the fore-runner of others and that they would be wise to make off.

Perhaps that was what happened ; perhaps the tremendous losses we had inflicted upon them made them come to the conclusion that they had better obtain reinforcements before attacking again. In any case, in the grey light of the dawn, with the aeroplane circling and hovering over-head, we saw the white-robed figures of the enemy slinking away among the rocks of the gorge.

Cheering, we leapt to our feet and sped them on their way with a volley. They answered with cries of defiance and a burst of firing.

We were safe ! My luck had held ! I was still alive and ready to fight more battles for France.

Reaction came swiftly. We flung ourselves down where we stood, too weary to move. Even the captain lay staring into space. The task of guarding the fortress was left to the colonial troops.

Then at last we began to stir again. There were the wounded to be tended and work to be done.

Our casualties had been appalling. Of the seven hundred men who had formed the garrison of the fortress, more than half were dead. The Legion's losses were the heaviest. There were only thirty-five of us, including the captain, fit for duty. The rest were either dead or wounded.

Mercifully, in that fierce hand-to-hand fighting there were more dead than wounded. The latter suffered agonies—and we could do nothing for them except bind up their wounds.

It was afternoon when the advance guard of the relief column arrived. We received them in silence, too weary and sick at heart to take any interest in them. They were only intruders. The battle was over.

Only the captain expressed his opinion of the higher command at Damascus in a welter of oaths. The commander of the relief column expressed his disgust with an eloquent shrug of his shoulders.

Nothing had been done to clear away the grisly refuse of the battle. The dead were still lying in heaps; blood and grime were everywhere.

A great grave was dug outside the walls and in this the dead legionnaires were buried with full military honours, the rest of us firing a volley over them. Of course, there was nothing in the nature of a religious service, but some of us, maybe, muttered a crude sort of a prayer for the souls of our pals who had gone.

The black troops were still half-mad with

terror, and it was necessary to drive them out of the fortress with whips and force them to dig a grave for their dead. It was pitiful to see them cringing under the whips and glancing apprehensively in the direction of the rocks, as if they expected to see the enemy come charging upon them.

Late in the evening the good news came that the remnants of the Fourth Squadron of the Legion were to proceed to Damascus, leaving the defence of Rashaya in the hands of the relief column and the colonials. The captain called us together and helped us celebrate it with an extra ration of rum.

It was as well, I think, that we were being relieved, for there would inevitably have been a fight between him and the commander of the relief column, who was one of those precise, "parade ground" officers, utterly incapable of understanding our skipper's unconventional methods.

At dawn the little band of thirty-five survivors rode out through the charred ruins of the fortress gates. We were laughing and singing like schoolboys off on a holiday.

We had been through hell—but there was a good time coming in Damascus!

CHAPTER X

DAMASCUS

DAMASCUS, that ancient city of dreams and romance, was still half-asleep when we approached it across the sun-baked desert. Yonder were some slow-moving Arab carts accompanied by dignified white-robed merchants. There, a pariah dog was slinking away.

It was a curious greeting that we received. After the way in which we had saved Rashaya it might have been expected that some sort of official welcome would have been given us. After all, we had achieved what very few troops in the world could accomplish. We had left a hundred dead behind us, heroes every one of them, no matter what their past had been. We, thirty-five blood-stained, war-weary men, had proved that we could carry out our bargain to serve France with honour and fidelity.

But it was too early for the generals and others of the high command to be out of their beds. And we were only the Foreign Legion.

It was left to a few lounging French soldiers, the Arabs, and the beggars to welcome us.

The soldiers jeered at us from the pavements, not even taking the trouble to remove their cigarettes from their mouths or to salute the captain. "The bandits are here!" I heard one say. "Look to your pockets!"

Arab mothers ran to drag their children away from us. "Look not on them!" they cried. "They are demons!" The beggars drew their filthy rags about them and spat as we passed.

We were the Legion, the scum!

I was riding near the captain and I could see the indignation that was blazing in his eyes. Somebody was going to hear about this—and the captain was probably going to be reprimanded for his pains!

He was a wonderful man. He was a born fighter and a glorious leader. He was capable of the most fiendish cruelties. But he loved the Legion. He would have made it the finest fighting force in the world. Whatever success we had achieved was due to him and to him alone.

But the authorities, so far as I could see, regarded him as a hopelessly eccentric nuisance. They would have been relieved, I think, to have heard that he had been killed. There was certainly little chance of his obtaining the promotion he deserved.

As we clattered along the streets a queer idea came to me. I wanted to suggest to the captain that we should escape together. I wanted to ask him why we should fling away our lives for the sake of a country that treated us in this way.

Of course, it remained nothing more than an idea. If I had suggested such a thing the captain would probably have blown my brains out.

But our welcome at Damascus increased my determination to escape a hundredfold. I had been lured into the Legion by cynical promises which had never been fulfilled. In return for my promises to serve for five years, I was being treated as a galley slave. I could win victories for France against desperate odds and in spite of gross mismanagement. I could do all the dirty work. And in return France regarded me as offal for the jackals to squabble over, something for the beggars to spit at.

At the first opportunity I was going to escape.

Later in the day we were paraded and inspected by a general, who gabbled off a speech and decorated our standard with a Croix de Guerre and two palms. The proceedings, however, were distinctly formal. I think some of the captain's remarks had reached the ears of the high command. He was capable of telling the most imposing "brass hat" what he thought of him.

There was a large draft awaiting us at Damascus, but the captain saw to it that those of us who had come back with him from Rashaya had plenty of free time. We needed it. We had a lot of back pay to draw and spend. We had also a very considerable quantity of loot to exchange into cash—and ultimately *vin rouge* and other joys—including that which had been collected by our dead comrades.

On the first evening Georgia, a Belgian, and myself, our pockets bulging with francs, set off to explore Damascus. After wandering about the streets for a time we discovered a really swagger café. It was the finest sight I had seen since I left London.

"This looks good," I remarked. "I think we ought to have one here !"

In we marched and, going up to the bar, I put down my money and ordered three bottles of wine.

The bar-tender looked us up and down and sniffed. "We don't serve legionnaires here," he said. His manner was about as genial as that of the head-waiter at the "Carlton" on being asked by a tramp for a cup of cocoa.

I was in no mood for that sort of treatment. "You don't eh? Well, here are three you're going to serve! And if you're not on the look-out for trouble you'll keep a civil tongue in your head!" There were several French officers sitting at the tables in the café and some of them rose to their feet with the intention, evidently, of ordering us out of the place.

In the mood we were in there was every prospect of our finding ourselves in the cells with a charge of striking an officer hanging over our heads.

Providence, however, came to our aid. Our captain happened to be in the café.

"What's the trouble, Harvey?" he asked, coming over to us.

"This son of a swine refuses to serve us because we're legionnaires, sir."

"What!" roared the captain, turning to the bar-tender.

It was as if a bomb had exploded. The bar-tender looked as if he was going to drop.

"Serve these boys with what they want!" ordered the captain. "If you don't, I'll nail your skin over the door!"

That bar-tender jumped to it. His one ambition in life was to serve the gentlemen of the Legion.

The other officers resumed their seats, mumbling

and muttering indignantly amongst themselves. They did not consider it prudent, however, to argue with the captain.

The latter stood us a round of drinks and stayed for some minutes chatting with us. He then went back to the table where he had been sitting before our arrival.

"If there's any more trouble, refer them to me," he said.

After a few drinks at the bar we went across to one of the tables and ordered a real dinner complete from *hors d'œuvres* to coffee and liqueurs.

It seemed the limit of luxury after the bully beef and biscuits which had been our staple fare at Rashaya. Even the French idea of a cigar seemed comparable with the finest Corona.

There was a dance-hall connected with the café, and after dinner we strolled in, feeling on very good terms with ourselves and the world in general. The band was playing a fox-trot.

"Georgia," I said, linking my arm in his, "this is the life!"

He nodded as he smilingly surveyed the group of dancing partners—Syrian girls mostly—who had been provided by the management.

"There's a peach!" he said, singling out the prettiest of the girls.

"Steady on !" I protested jokingly as he stepped towards her. "I saw her first !"

The girl laughed ; she had wonderful gazelle-like eyes. "You speak English ?" she asked.

"I am English," I answered.

"Good ! I speak English. American mission at Beyrout teach me. I dance with you because you are an Englishman."

And, nestling in my arms, she whirled me into the dance, leaving Georgia gazing after us.

He soon found a partner, however, and appeared to get on very well with her. Indeed, after three or four dances Georgia and his partner disappeared, and it was three o'clock in the morning before he returned to the barracks.

My little partner was a charming, cuddly kid. She had all the simplicity of the savage beneath a very thin veneer of civilization. She must have been a good dancer, too, for she steered me through waltzs, fox-trots and one-steps without mishap ; she even did her best to teach me the tango.

She was immensely proud of her proficiency in English and wanted to know all about the "bloodthirsty Legion", as she called it ; why I had joined, whether I was going to escape,

what had happened at Rashaya, how long I was
going to stay at Damascus, and innumerable other
questions.

She had a tremendous admiration for the
English, believed that they were all millionaires,
and wished that they would come and drive the
French out of Damascus.

"You don't like the French ?" I asked.

She screwed up her pretty little nose. "They
are a dirty lot of swine," she answered with
piquant downrightness. "But the English are
gentlemen."

Perhaps her friendliness was genuine. On the
other hand, it was equally possible that she was
a spy for the Druses. It did not matter, for I had
no information of any value to divulge. And I was
much too grateful for her companionship and
sympathy to bother. She made me feel almost
civilized again.

Superior people, I'm afraid, would not have
considered her a nice girl. She had a fondness
for Benedictine. And she was quite frank about
the fact that she combined another and much
older profession with that of a dance-partner.
She regarded it as a matter of course. She even
gave me some illuminating sidelights on the habits
of French officers.

But to me she remained the essence of feminine daintiness.

"You will come with me?" she asked at the end of the evening.

I have never posed as a saint. I was in a devil-may-care mood after the horrors of Rashaya, and I had had more than enough to drink. And God knows she was pretty enough to tempt St. Anthony himself.

But I couldn't forget what she had said about the French being a dirty lot of swine and the English being gentlemen. I felt that it was up to me to justify her illusions. And I wanted to thank her for her companionship, for having made me feel that I was something more than a blood-stained brute.

"It would spoil the evening," I answered, shaking my head.

She gazed at me in a puzzled way, obviously amazed at my refusal. She had assumed from the start that the evening would end in what was to her the conventional way. Then the glimmer of understanding came into her eyes.

"You are English," she said with a nod. "You are different from the French pigs. You are a gentleman. You will come and see me again? I will watch for you."

"I'll be here to-morrow evening, kid," I promised.

I held my head very high when I walked back to the barracks. I was immensely proud of the fact that I was an English gentleman. And I spent most of the night dreaming of romance in which the little Syrian girl figured as the heroine and I as a chivalrous knight-errant.

Perhaps I was a fool. Perhaps it was merely the effects of the drink I had had.

My romance had a nasty shock the next day. Some of the officers who had not dared to argue the point with our captain had evidently complained to the authorities about our intrusion into that very select café. A notice was posted up informing us that the café was out of bounds to men of the Legion.

Naturally we were very indignant. And we were even more indignant that evening after we had had drinks at the low-class haunts of the town.

I don't know whether it was Georgia or I who made the mad suggestion that we ought to assert our independence. In any case, the two of us presented ourselves at the forbidden café late at night and forced our way in. We were both drunk enough to be reckless and we were very demonstrative. Nobody had a chance of overlooking the fact that we had arrived.

Within a few moments a real "rough house" was in progress. Waiters and everybody else employed in the café rushed forward to assist in the task of turning us out. We met them with our fists, knocking them sprawling. Tables were overturned, glasses and bottles smashed. Georgia, by way of adding to the excitement, managed to put out half the lights. All the people in the dance-hall came crowding forward to see what was the cause of the disturbance. An equally curious throng pressed in from the street.

Having let off a good deal of steam I grabbed Georgia by the arm and suggested that, if we wanted to avoid serious trouble, we had better disappear from the scene as quickly as possible. But it was more difficult to get out of the café than into it, and it was not long before it began to look as if we were going to be cornered. We should have to surrender and then be ignominiously marched off to the cells.

Then suddenly I noticed my little Syrian girl. We dashed across to her.

Taking me by the hand, she led us through a door, down a passage, and out into a regular network of narrow alleys, finally setting us on the road to the barracks.

"Run!" she cried. "And then nobody will be

able to discover that it was you who were at the café."

We arrived at the barracks doing our best to look very innocent indeed. Nothing was said about the affair that night ; no corporal came to blackguard us in the morning. We began to congratulate ourselves on the prospect of escaping the consequences of our night out. Then the captain sent for us.

For some moments he surveyed us in silence.

"Well, you two beauties," he said at length, "it may interest you to know that you owe me five hundred francs."

"Five hundred francs, sir ?"

"Yes, that is what it has cost me to keep last night's escapade from the general's ears."

He then went on to call us every variety of fool—emphasizing his remarks with a wealth of cosmopolitan oaths—but he did not ask us for the five hundred francs.

And I never saw my little Syrian girl again.

Perhaps she still thinks sometimes of the legionnaire who was also "an English gentleman". I am still grateful to her for having made the mistake.

Georgia and I laid low after that, confining our attention to the various dens which were

available for the Legion without incurring the
displeasure of our superiors. These haunts of the
underworld are much the same everywhere and
are not nearly so thrilling in reality as in fiction.
They were inhabited chiefly by thieves, cut-throats
and touts for brothels. The great point in their
favour was that a man could get thoroughly
drunk quickly and cheaply, and so forget the
squalor of his surroundings.

The other chief excitement was an occasional
attempt to knife us in some dark alley. These
murders and attempted murders were a frequent
occurrence, and in the labyrinth of dark and
narrow streets it was seldom that the assassin
was captured. The authorities were very energetic
with patrols of gendarmes and soldiers, but these
were hampered by the fact that the sympathy
of the inhabitants was wholly with the murderers.
To kill a European was the normal local method
of expressing dissatisfaction with the French
régime.

One evening Georgia and I had an uncomfortably
exciting adventure in this connection. We were
returning to barracks, not altogether sober, when
two Arabs approached us down the dark, deserted
street.

Fortunately we were not so drunk as to be

entirely unsuspecting. The Arabs sprang at us as they passed, whipping their knives from under their burnouses. We leapt aside. My man missed altogether and I greeted him with a thump in the ribs which made him grunt. The other was a little more successful, and Georgia received a slight wound in the fleshy part of the shoulder. Without making any further attempt the Arabs turned and fled.

If we had been sober and sensible we would have congratulated ourselves on our escape and continued on our way to the barracks. But unfortunately we were drunk enough to be reckless. Georgia, moreover, was thoroughly annoyed about that scratch on the shoulder. Pulling out our revolvers, we dashed in pursuit, Georgia a few yards ahead of me.

As we raced along Georgia fired a couple of shots at the white figures fleeing before us, but the only result was to increase their speed. Through the silence of the night they fled before us like ghosts, darting down this alley and up that.

The distance between us was steadily increasing. Sobered by the exertion I called to Georgia, who was still a yard or two ahead of me, that we had better give up the chase. I realized that at any moment we might find ourselves called upon to deal with a dozen or so of our would-be assassins' friends—and in our present pumped condition we would stand very little chance of getting away with our lives. Georgia, however, was not in the mood to listen to reason. He was determined to avenge that scratch on the shoulder and his only answer was a breathless curse and another shot from his revolver.

Suddenly the Arabs darted through an open doorway. Georgia, utterly reckless of consequences, sprinted forward. Expecting every instant to hear the door slammed, I sprinted too, trying to keep up with him.

The Arabs, however, did not pause in their flight to close the door behind them. Then, as Georgia turned to dash into the house, he tripped and fell. A moment later I stumbled over him and we were both sprawling in the roadway.

That fall saved our lives. Immediately inside the doorway and within a foot of our noses was an open trap-door. If we had rushed into that house we should inevitably have plunged through the trap into the cellar below—and there would have been another addition to the mysteries of Damascus.

The realization that only chance had saved us from certain death cooled even Georgia's ardour.

We picked ourselves up, rubbed our bruises, and decided that the best thing we could do was to return to barracks.

We then found that we were lost, and we spent the better part of two hours wandering about the alleys until at length we found a street that we recognized in the darkness. The sergeant of the guard welcomed us with a flood of abuse for being out so late.

We reported the matter in the morning, but we were unable to find our bearings again and, so far as I know, the house with the trap-door was never discovered.

But Georgia and I chased no more Arabs.

The red lamp industry, of course, flourished in Damascus—it was the one thing that the French seemed capable of organizing efficiently. In the interests of discipline the various establishments were divided into three classes, their patrons being officers, N.C.O.s, and other ranks respectively. The first class undoubtedly looked the most inviting from the outside and presumably housed the most charming and accomplished ladies. It was a serious crime for a private to attempt to patronize a brothel of the wrong class. I don't think there was any danger of an officer being tempted to sample the wares in one of the establishments reserved for the other ranks. In any case, I never heard of such a thing happening.

The medical inspection was made regularly once a week, the doctor being a plump, jolly little man who was seemingly entirely unaffected by his job, which some people, to say the least, would have found somewhat nauseating. According to the barrack-room gossips he made the fullest possible use of his position—and never paid. As the captain's batman, I must certainly admit that he had the biggest fund of indecent stories of any man I have ever heard. And there were a few strong ones told in the Legion !

After their experiences at Rashaya, and having back pay and loot to spend, the legionnaires were enthusiastic patrons of the red lamp, and a good deal of the barrack-room talk was taken up with frank discussions on the comparative charms of various girls. Often these arguments resulted in fights ending in somebody being taken to the hospital or the cells. On one occasion a Sicilian knifed a comrade for maintaining that he stood first in the affections of a certain lady. As the lady in question was available for anyone who cared to pay the requisite fee, it seemed rather absurd to treat the matter so seriously.

Every evening a patrol visited the cafés and

brothels to maintain order and to ensure that pleasure-seekers returned to barracks by the proper hour. Its methods were rough and ready, the N.C.O. in charge usually enforcing his directions with the aid of his boot or whip. The Legion, however, was seldom called upon to provide this patrol—its members had an unfortunate habit of forgetting their duties as temporary policemen and of joining the revellers whom they were supposed to be shepherding. On the other hand, they certainly added a hundredfold to the anxieties of the patrol during their stay in Damascus.

On one occasion the hag in charge of one of the brothels reported that two of her best girls were missing. It being no part of the patrol's duty to look for lost prostitutes no notice was taken of the matter. Then, some time after, news came that two girls were being murdered in a certain house by a couple of French soldiers.

On breaking into the house the patrol discovered two legionnaires, Rylev and Maletski—Russians of the very worst type whose habits were a byword even in the Legion. They were armed with whips, and with them were the two missing girls, stark naked and their bodies covered with the weals of the whips.

These two beauties were confined to barracks for the rest of their stay in Damascus. They were enormously proud of their exploit, however, and regaled the rest of us with a detailed description of the "entertainment" which they had forced their victims to provide.

And nobody appeared to be disgusted. It was just life—according to Foreign Legion standards.

Romance at Damascus was not wholly of the red lamp order. There was the case of Verlozzi.

Verlozzi was the Don Juan of the squadron. Tall, dark, and extraordinarily handsome, he was one of those debonair and plausible scoundrels with a tremendous power over women. He was all the more dangerous because he was utterly unscrupulous. It was this combination which doubtless explained his presence in the Legion.

He took immense pains with his appearance, even in the desert, and seldom got drunk like the rest of us. More out of vanity than friendliness he used to yarn to us for hours about his amorous adventures in the past. On the other hand, he was a good soldier and had proved it at Rashaya.

Verlozzi, in short, was just the type of suave and handsome blackguard who could persuade an innocent and trusting girl that he was really a hero who had been sadly misused by Fate. There was nobody who could "tell the tale" more convincingly.

One evening Verlozzi returned looking even more pleased with himself than usual, and on being asked the cause of it announced that he had "got off" with a colonel's wife.

"What's the matter with the general's daughter?" asked someone incredulously.

Verlozzi, however, not only stuck to his story but provided us with details. The colonel was a pompous, dull, and elderly member of the general staff. The wife was a perfect peach, nearly forty years younger than her husband, whom she had married, without her own wishes being in any way consulted, shortly after leaving the convent where she had been educated.

Verlozzi had noticed her before and was fully conscious of the fact that she had always gazed after him, wondering doubtless who was this handsome Romeo in the uniform of the "blood-thirsty Legion". He had introduced himself to her by the simple expedient of asking her whether it was her handkerchief that he had just picked up. It was not, because he had previously bought the handkerchief in a shop.

The girl in a shy, tentative sort of way had asked

him about himself. With all the fervour of an imitation Romeo he had told her of the terrible hardships he had to endure in the Legion, of the degraded company he had to suffer. She could imagine what agony it must be for a man, like himself, of a sensitive nature and noble birth. What he missed most of all was the companionship of pure and sympathetic womanhood. This was the first time for many weary months that he had spoken to a woman belonging to the world he had renounced.

"You should have seen her swallow the dope!" said Verlozzi with his sleek self-satisfied smile. "There were tears in her eyes; bless her little heart!"

She had asked him why he had joined the Legion. He had replied with the old and trusty gag about suffering for another's sin.

She had offered to speak to her husband, to see if he could do anything to ameliorate the bitter lot of this ill-used hero. He had refused, saying that he preferred to meet his fate with the fortitude becoming to a true Verlozzi.

Then he had coaxed the conversation round to the subject of the lady herself, getting her to talk of her dull, pompous and unsympathetic husband, of her loveless marriage. Deftly he had insinuated that she also was an innocent victim of circumstance and that things might have been very different— if only they had met in the old happy days when he had lived in the ancestral castle.

At length they had parted. The girl had hinted that perhaps they would meet again. But Verlozzi had shaken his head in his best Sydney Carton manner. It could not be. They belonged to different worlds. She was a colonel's wife ; he was merely a trooper in the Legion of the Damned. But he would treasure her in his memory for ever— the angel of Damascus who had smiled on him. Even in the nethermost depths of hell he would remember her.

Verlozzi winked.

"She's crying her eyes out over me," he prophesied. "When next she sees her husband she'll think what a dull, uninteresting fool he is compared with me, and how little he appreciates her. She'll dream all night about me and to-morrow she'll be determined to meet me again. The little peach ! I know how to manage her !"

And probably he was right.

Of course, the girl was a fool and yet she could not be blamed. She was young and inexperienced. She had left the sheltered existence of a convent school to marry a man forty years older than herself. She had been starved of romance. How could she know that this apparently ill-used hero was nothing more than a smooth-tongued blackguard ?

It was not the first time that it had occurred to me that in this life the cunning and unscrupulous have a most unfair advantage over the innocent and trusting.

The girl doubtless believed every word Verlozzi had told her, and thought that she had discovered one of those romantic heroes with whom popular novelists people the Legion. Her only thought was to show a little human kindliness to a man who had suffered cruelly at the hands of Fate. It never entered her head that she was playing with fire, that he was a swine seeking to drag her down to his own level.

Soon Verlozzi's romance became the chief topic of conversation among the rank and file of the squadron. Most of them regarded it as a huge joke, and their only regret was that they had neither the cunning nor the good looks to be able to follow his example. In their opinion a woman's sole purpose was to be a plaything.

There were times, however, when I noticed Georgia's lips twitching. He, the only man of really noble birth amongst us, could remember a time when a woman had meant something more than a plaything.

But we could do nothing—unless perhaps we had murdered Verlozzi.

I saw the girl on one or two occasions. She looked exquisitely fragrant in her beautifully-cut gown. A tall, slender, perfectly bred flower. The sort of woman on whom the ordinary man looks with humble reverence.

Verlozzi kept us well posted with the progress of his romance. Their clandestine meetings became a daily event. Soon she was giving him presents of money, cigarettes and cigars. And always on his return Verlozzi gave us a detailed description of all that had happened, how cleverly he had told the tale, and how unsuspectingly she had believed him. Within a week he was boasting that she was completely infatuated with him and that he could do anything he liked with her.

"I can see it in her eyes," he said with his sleek smile. "A woman's eyes never lie—if only you know how to read them!"

Then at last came the climax of Verlozzi's machinations. Her husband was to be away from home for the evening and she invited Verlozzi to visit her in secret. She wanted to give him a little dinner—to remind him of the old days when he had been an Italian nobleman.

Verlozzi was in great form when he returned that night. Smoking one of the colonel's cigars, he told how he had slipped in at her window; how she had served him to the exquisite meal which she had prepared with her own dainty hands for fear of arousing the suspicions of the servants; how he had seen to it that she had taken her full share of the champagne; how he had taken her in his arms and kissed her hair, her eyes, her lips; how he had carried her into the bedroom. There was nothing omitted.

His audience roared with appreciative laughter. Thanks to Verlozzi, the Legion was having its revenge on one of those brass hats! It was the best joke they had ever heard!

The next evening, as debonair and gallant as ever, Verlozzi set forth to continue his romance. But his comrades waited in vain for him to return and give them more of those intimately detailed accounts of his amorous exploits. They wondered whether this prince of cads had eloped with the girl.

In the morning, however, Verlozzi's body was found in one of the streets with an Arab knife stuck between the shoulders.

Apparently it was another of those midnight outrages perpetrated by the natives. Another Syrian had expressed his dissatisfaction with France. On the other hand, it may be that the plump and pompous colonel knew what had happened. Perhaps rumours had reached his ears ; perhaps he had returned home unexpectedly and discovered the Don Juan of the Legion ; perhaps the murderer was in his pay.

No inquiry was made, and it was left to the Legion to argue over to our hearts' content. The same day we heard the news that the colonel's wife had committed suicide.

Another romance of the Foreign Legion had come to its appointed conclusion !

In Damascus we were more or less in touch with civilization and newspapers were available. It was glorious to get hold of an out-of-date English paper and read it from beginning to end, advertisements and all. It was like a breath of fresh air to learn that Hobbs was still making centuries and Steve Donoghue still riding winners. I confess to stealing one of those papers and carrying it about with me, reading it in my odd moments until I knew it practically by heart. To me it was the greatest literature in the world.

And I used to browse over it, dreaming

of all the wonderful things that were going to happen when I escaped and got back to England.

One afternoon Carlos, a Portuguese, brought in a paper containing the picture of a well-known continental dancer who had recently married a millionaire from South Africa. After asking us what we thought of her, he went on to describe her as the blackest-hearted Jezebel that ever played the devil's business, illuminating his remarks with several lurid incidents from her career. When we asked him how he came to know so much about her, he answered that he happened to be her husband.

It was immediately suggested that here was an opportunity for blackmail which ought not to be missed. The whole squadron was ready to share in the good fortune of Carlos's wife.

Carlos spent the rest of the afternoon concocting a letter in which he felicitated the lady on her second venture into matrimony, and suggested that as she now had a millionaire's banking account at her disposal she might find it convenient to send a few thousand francs to her first and legal husband.

The letter was duly dispatched, but we left Damascus before the answer had time to arrive.

And in the next battle Carlos had the misfortune to be killed.

It was not usual in the Legion for the dead to be mourned; it was accepted as a normal incident. But there was genuine regret for Carlos among those who had been looking forward to helping him squander his share of the millions of his wife's second husband. And there was a lot of grumbling about the way in which Fate interfered with matters which she ought to leave alone.

There was one man, Doiser, who never took any interest in women. He did not patronize the red lamp establishments, or glance appreciatively after the Syrian girls, or even talk about the other sex. He was regarded by the others as being hopelessly eccentric, and innumerable more or less libellous stories were told about him. He did not care, but merely shrugged his shoulders in his stolid way. His attitude was all the more irritating because he was not openly antagonistic to women and never indulged in any cynical remarks on the subject. He simply was not interested.

At last half a dozen of the wilder spirits decided that it was time for practical steps to be taken for completing Doiser's education. They accordingly visited one of the red lamp places, told the ladies there all about Doiser and his peculiarities, and promised them all sorts of rewards if they succeeded in making a man of him. They also arranged for a number of spy-holes to be made in the wall and door, so that they could see the fun.

One evening the plotters kidnapped Doiser in a dark alley, blindfolding him and binding him hand and foot. They then carried him to the *maison de tolerance* and locked him in with the assembled ladies who had promised to "do their damnedest".

Even the plotters had to admit that the result was a complete triumph for Doiser. The girls, we gathered, had indeed done their best ; St. Anthony himself would have been unable to withstand their alluring blandishments. But Doiser had merely shrugged his shoulders and politely requested that the door should be unlocked.

The only possible explanation was that Doiser was a freak.

It was some time later, during the battle of Scueida, that I learnt the truth about Doiser. I chanced to see him lying wounded and, noticing that he was fumbling weakly at his tunic, I went over to him to do what I could for him. He had been shot through the chest and I knew at a glance that there was no hope for him.

"Harvey," he gasped as I knelt beside him, "you might—get the—the miniature—out of my tunic——"

Undoing his tunic, I found that he was wearing round his neck a miniature portrait of a girl, blue-eyed, fair-haired, and smiling.

"Thanks," he muttered as I placed it in his hands.

For some moments he gazed at it with his fast-glazing eyes. Then he glanced up at me.

"Bury it with me, Harvey," he whispered. "Don't let the others see it—don't tell them about—her——"

He died with his eyes fixed on the portrait of the girl whose memory was so precious to him that it would have been desecration even for her existence to have been known to the blackguards of the Legion.

Sometimes I have wondered who she was and what was the story behind that miniature. And yet I have always felt rather ashamed of my curiosity. What right have we to prowl and pry among the secrets of the dead?

The squadron, meanwhile, had been brought up to full strength by means of another draft from Sousse—the usual tough crowd drawn from all parts of the world—and we were ready to carry on with the work of winning the war against the

Druses. All sorts of rumours as to our next destination were in circulation, but, as the captain's batman, I was in a position to obtain more or less reliable information. It was the captain himself who told me one morning that we should be leaving Damascus in three days' time.

"There's going to be a real battle," he added. "A first-class affair."

I can't say that I was particularly thrilled by the news. Having no quarrel with the Druses, I was not anxious to kill any more of them, and I knew that, no matter whether the forthcoming battle was first, second, or third class, the dirtiest work would inevitably fall to the lot of the Legion. However, there was some comfort in the thought that in a real battle we should presumably have some more reliable support than the black colonial troops, and also that we should have at any rate an adequate supply of ammunition. I was not anxious to repeat the Rashaya experience.

I was discussing the news with some of the others when it was suggested that, as we still had some money left, it would be a good idea to indulge in a real "beano" by way of a finale to our stay in Damascus. The idea was taken up with enthusiasm, and then somebody suggested that we might invite the captain.

Many were dubious about this, especially the recent arrivals from Sousse. In the Legion officers as a class are not regarded as people to be encouraged. And there were officers who would have regarded such an invitation as an insult, and would have answered it by knocking the bearer down, or giving him a cut with a riding whip. But our captain was different. On dozens of occasions, in battle and on rest, he had proved that in addition to being our leader he was one of ourselves. Those of us who had returned from Rashaya carried the day, and I was deputed to invite the captain to the feast.

"Do you want me, Harvey?" he asked when I told him the news.

"If we didn't, we shouldn't invite you, sir," I answered.

He nodded. "Very well, I'm coming," he said. "And you can tell the boys that they've made me the proudest man in the French Army."

After that, of course, we invited the lieutenant, and all the N.C.O.s as well. They all accepted.

It was a great evening. We took over one of the cafés for the occasion. The menu, perhaps, was on the plain and homely side, but it was satisfying, and there were barrels of wine.

And the captain did not merely drop in and

survey the gathering in a dignified sort of way. He saw the whole thing through from beginning to end. He was one of us, drinking and roaring out the choruses.

I don't suppose such a thing has ever happened before in the Legion. The disciplinarians would have been terribly shocked. But we were all too drunk to worry about them—though in all probability the affair reached the ears of the authorities and another black mark was entered in the captain's record !

At the end I climbed on to a table and started singing "For He's a Jolly Good Fellow". Not half a dozen of the others understood the words, but after a few moments they all guessed what the sentiment was. The jumped to their feet and roared out the old song—or as near to it as they could manage—cheering the skipper to the echo.

Then he stood up and saluted us—the scum of the Legion !

He was a man in a million !

CHAPTER XI

EZRA AND SCUEIDA

AT the end of our rest in Damascus we proceeded to Ezra, a tiny desert post lying only some seventy miles from the Palestine frontier.

And Palestine was under British protection. Once across that frontier I would be safe. It was a tempting thought, and I spent a good deal of time gazing across the desert and wondering if there was any hope of my being able to accomplish those seventy miles without being caught.

I decided that as a lone adventure it was impossible. I should need food, water, and other supplies. There were other posts between us and the frontier. It would be wiser to wait until we were nearer the frontier, and it would be better to have a trustworthy companion. The affair needed careful planning. A mere wild dash would inevitably end in failure.

It soon became apparent that there was serious

business afoot. Troops of all sorts came pouring into Ezra—Moroccan and Tunisian Spahis, Tirailleurs, blacks, and even some artillery. It was quite a treat to see some 75's again—we could have done with a battery at Rashaya.

The news soon leaked out. We were going to attack Scueida, the last big town held by the Druses. Some of the new arrivals were quite excited about it ; after their months at Sousse they were glad of the prospect of seeing some fighting at last. Personally, I had had all the fighting I wanted during the past few months, and had seen enough blood spilt to last me a lifetime.

I was not afraid ; I had rubbed shoulders with Death too long for that. I was simply nauseated by the whole business. Again and again I found myself thinking of that hideous scene at Rashaya when the captain had murdered the prisoners in cold blood and afterwards laid delirious for days in his fetid, blood-caked clothes. I remembered the massacre of the women and children at Tel-y-Ded.

These were the memories which kept forcing themselves uppermost in my mind. I found myself wondering what further horrors awaited me in the future.

I wanted to get away and forget.

We had been at Ezra about a week when the captain sent for me and told me that I was to accompany Sergeant Crukov on a reconnoitring patrol. This was a distinct honour, for only the most reliable men were chosen for this work. Moreover, the sergeant, a grim and dour man who had once been an officer in the Russian Army, was probably the finest scout in Syria. The others all congratulated me on my good fortune. And indeed I was glad to have the job. It meant a change and the prospect of adventure.

It was also, perhaps, a sign that the captain had marked me out for promotion. But non-commissioned rank no longer attracted me. I had long since forgotten those dazzling dreams of the day when I should go to the military college at St. Cyr and emerge a fully-fledged officer of the Legion. Reality had destroyed those fond visions of the days when I had been an innocent inquirer at the French consulate.

Carrying three days' rations, the sergeant and I set off at four o'clock the following morning. For a couple of hours we trotted in silence across the desert, then the sergeant nodded towards some small hillocks lying ahead of us.

"See those rocks?" he said. "Make a half-mile detour and see what's behind them."

It was quite pleasant to hear him speak. I galloped off and, leaving my horse at the foot of the rocks, crept forward and scanned the horizon through my field-glasses. There was nothing to be seen.

On my return the sergeant received the information with a nod and we set off again. The sun was now beating mercilessly upon us and the glare was blinding. I was more than glad when, towards midday, we approached a ruined village.

Leaving me in charge of the horses, the sergeant went forward to investigate. Finding all clear; he signalled to me to come forward.

"We'll stay here in the shade until the evening," he said. "Then we'll push on towards the hills."

After watering the horses at a pool we had a meal ourselves and then settled down to rest, taking it in turns to keep guard whilst the other slept. This siesta was more for the horses' sakes than for our own; we had to keep them fresh, for our lives might depend on their speed on the return journey.

As I watched the sleeping sergeant I realized

that, from some point of view, this was a Heaven-
sent opportunity for escaping. The sergeant and
I had six days' rations between us and two of the
best horses in the squadron. We were not expected
back at Ezra for three days and by then I would
be across the frontier and in Palestine. Even if
I had the bad luck to be caught it would be easy
enough to concoct a tale about a desperate fight
with the enemy, the sergeant having been killed,
and I having lost my bearings in the desert—such
things had been known to happen to lone patrols.
And if my luck held it would not even be known
that I had escaped. It would be assumed at
Ezra that the patrol had been scuppered by the
Druses.

It was a splendid opportunity, but it had one
defect. It entailed murdering the sergeant. I had
become hardened to bloodshed during the past
few months and had no undue respect for human
life. But I had not yet sunk so low as to be
capable of murdering a sleeping man in cold
blood.

When the sun was low we started off again and
reached the range of low, rock-strewn hills just
at nightfall. Tethering our horses in a large cave,
we climbed to the top of the hills and saw in the
darkness which covered the plain before us the

lights of the enemy's camp. Of course it was impossible to form any opinion of their numbers, but it was obvious that they were in considerable force.

We returned to the cave to await the dawn, taking it in turns to sleep and watch.

"No cigarettes," said the sergeant as he curled up on the floor of the cave. "A lighted cigarette can be seen for miles in the darkness here in the desert. And we don't want to call attention to ourselves."

"Right you are, sergeant," I answered.

He was not what might be called a talkative man, but what he said was to the point. And he certainly inspired confidence.

In the morning he left me to guard the horses in the cave whilst he went to learn what he could about the enemy.

"I don't expect to be long," he said. "If I'm not back by nightfall make for Ezra and give this note to the captain."

Handing me the note, he strode away.

Left to myself, I stood for some time at the entrance to the cave. It was a huge affair and the two horses were completely hidden in its recesses. There was nothing to be seen—just the eternal desert, the sun steadily rising in the heavens, and an odd vulture or two. After a time I went back into the cave and groomed the horses, watered and fed them. Then, sitting down on the floor of the cave I wondered how the sergeant was getting on and ruminated on things in general.

Suddenly I heard some stones rattle near the entrance to the cave.

Instantly I was on my feet, every sense alert, my revolver in my hand. It might be that the sergeant had returned; on the other hand it might be less-welcome visitors. Prepared for anything, I crept cautiously forward.

An Arab was standing near the entrance to the cave. He had his back towards me and was gazing across the desert.

Gripping my revolver, I stood watching him from behind a rock. I dared not shoot him—he might have friends in the neighbourhood, and I did not want to attract their attention.

The minutes passed. Then he turned and, noticing the entrance to the cave, came towards me. I waited until he was almost upon me; then, springing forward, I caught him with the butt of my revolver between the eyes. Without a groan he dropped senseless to the ground. Dragging him further into the cave, I tied him up with a picketing rope. Then I went to the entrance to the cave and gazed anxiously around. There were no more Arabs to be seen, however, and nothing further happened until the sergeant returned. He was cursing under his breath and gripping his shoulder. There was blood on his tunic.

"Bind this up!" he growled. "They spotted me and one of them plugged me through the shoulder. The sooner we get started the better!"

As I was bandaging up his wound he noticed my prisoner. I told him what had happened.

He nodded in his taciturn way. "It would have been better to have used your knife," he said. "Dead men don't make any mistakes."

In a few moments we were ready to start.

"What shall we do about him?" I asked, nodding towards my prisoner.

"Leave him," answered the sergeant.

A few minutes later we were trotting off across the desert. The sergeant must have completely baffled the Druses who had spotted him, for not a shot was fired from the hills behind us. Probably they were searching for us in the opposite direction.

All went well until nightfall when suddenly a volley was fired on us from some rocks away on our right and a troop of horsemen came charging upon us.

"Follow me !" shouted the sergeant, digging his spurs into his horse.

Firing as they rode, the Arabs tried to intercept us. I was a little distance behind the sergeant and I managed to get one of our pursuers with a lucky shot from my revolver. But two of them nearly succeeded in cutting me off and I had to swerve in order to avoid them, emptying my revolver at them as I passed within a few yards.

Then in the darkness I lost sight of the sergeant. It could not be helped. I could only race blindly on, somewhere in the direction of Ezra, and trust to my horse to outpace my pursuers.

For some time they kept close at my heels, but gradually I drew away from them and at last they gave up the chase and I was able to give my horse a breather.

The next problem was to find my way back to camp ; I had only the vaguest notion of where it lay. Keeping my eye on the stars I jogged along for two or three hours when I saw some lights twinkling on the horizon. Changing my course, I trotted towards them.

Suddenly a shot was fired from about fifteen yards ahead and the bullet whistled past my ear.

Pulling my horse up on to his haunches and thinking that I had stumbled upon a Druse camp, I was on the point of wheeling and galloping away when the owner of the rifle shouted in an unmistakably African voice: *"Qui va la?"*

Having told that Senegalese sentry what I thought of him, I discovered that it was not Ezra but Gazalie, the next post, that I had struck. The next thing that happened was a French officer ordering me to be placed under arrest as a deserter. Fortunately, however, there was a telephone between Ezra and Gazalie, and the officer was able to obtain corroboration of my story. Instead of being sent to the guard-room, I was given a meal and a shake-down bed. Early the next morning I set off for Ezra, which I reached without any further adventure.

Sergeant Crukov had got back safely during the night and was already in hospital with his wounded shoulder.

I don't know whether any action was taken as a result of the information we brought back from that patrol. At any rate, no attack was made from Ezra on the camp we had discovered in the hills.

A few days later the column moved forward to the attack on Scueida. It was a most imposing business and there was no question of there being any shortage, either of men or stores, on this occasion. The explanation, possibly, lay in the fact that on this occasion the general himself was in command. This was no desperate defence of a desert outpost; it was a full-dress battle, the capture of an important town, and it was to be heralded throughout France as a great victory. There were cavalry, artillery, and infantry. Stores and transport covered a distance of three miles. There were six aeroplanes circling and hovering overhead.

The Druses, of course, had neither aeroplanes nor artillery. They had to rely upon their rifles and knives and inborn courage. The odds would have been overwhelmingly in our favour had it not been for the fact that the majority of our infantry were black colonial troops—and we had already learnt at Rashaya what was to be expected of them.

Progress was slow across the sun-scorched desert, and the march to Scueida occupied six days. Occasionally, the advance and flank guards had a little trouble with Druse snipers, but the main column had nothing in particular to do except keep moving and curse the heat and the desert. Being mounted, we had a comparatively easy time.

And the blacks, of course, were accustomed to the conditions. But the white infantry had a very trying time and scores of them broke down.

At length, soon after nightfall, we reached the position from which the attack was to be made. That was a busy night. The guns took up their positions for shelling the town; cavalry and infantry endeavoured to sort themselves out and to find the positions which they were supposed to occupy on the maps. There was all the confusion and swearing which is inevitable when the preparations for a big attack take place in the darkness and nobody has any idea as to where he is and what is happening.

The captain was in a fiendish temper. He was not at his best when playing a subordinate part in a civilized battle, with the usual chits arriving every few minutes from headquarters. He needed the independence and excitement of an honest, hand-to-hand scrap. And he did not take kindly to the task of answering questions about the number of troops under his command who had suffered from measles and how many tins of plum and apple jam he had in hand.

His opinion of the brass hats, and his language, grew steadily stronger. Several of the chits he threw away and refused to answer. And many of the unfortunate runners had to bolt precipitately from his presence, scared for their lives.

The Legion, we were informed, was to have the honour of being among the first to enter Scueida. Others sharing the honour were the black colonial troops. In other words, the riff-raff were being given the dirty work of the attack, and the "real soldiers" were being reserved for the ceremonial entry when the town had been captured and all was safe.

At last the dawn broke and Scueida could be seen before us looming out of the mists like a fairy citadel. Before it was a plain, broken by irregular fields, stone walls, and gullies. From these the enemy promptly opened fire upon us.

Almost immediately the guns in the rear opened out with an ear-splitting crash. Some swept the plain with a barrage of shrapnel; others poured high explosive shells into the doomed city. The aeroplanes, flying high, added to the work of destruction by dropping bombs.

The line advanced.

We had blacks on either flank. Their officers and N.C.O.s, as usual, were urging them forward with whips. The enemy maintained a fairly heavy rifle-fire and we suffered a few casualties.

Even the barrage and the knowledge that they were hopelessly outclassed could not break their fanatical courage.

I could not help feeling sorry for them, and rather ashamed of ourselves. We had fought them fair and square at Mesmie and Rashaya, but this was not playing the game. It was like setting an extraordinarily good feather-weight to tackle Gene Tunney. In my heart I hoped that the little man would win.

An occasional bullet whirring past my ear, however, kept my sympathies within bounds.

All went well until, away on our right, a body of Druses rose from a gully and charged upon the black Tirailleurs. Yelling their battle-cry and their swords flashing in the sun, they dashed madly forward.

Never have I seen men run as did those black Tirailleurs. They dropped their rifles and machine-guns, and, screaming with terror, turned and fled. Their officers and N.C.O.s chased after them, lashing them with their whips and shooting them down. But instead of stopping them this only added to their speed. The Syrian mile record was smashed to smithereens that morning.

To the captain it was a Heaven-sent opportunity. At last he could do something without

234

waiting for orders! Here was the chance for a real fight!

"Come on!" he yelled, digging his spurs into his horse. "Give the swine hell!"

He was himself again!

Technically, I suppose, he exceeded his orders and committed various other military crimes. But he didn't worry about that.

We met the Druses in a terrific shock and for ten mad minutes we fought in a whirlwind of swords and knives; cutting, hacking, thrusting, slashing; man to man. It was the real thing!

We wiped them out, everyone of them. Some troops were rushed forward from the rear, the line reformed and the advance began again.

I was given the job of liaison orderly, and had to keep galloping backwards and forwards and to and fro with messages. It was an exciting business for I made an excellent target for the enemy snipers. Bullets flicked the sand beneath the hoofs of my horse, which was prancing about like a ballet dancer. Others whistled past me or spattered against the rocks. Once I thought they had got me when I felt a sharp pain by my eye. But it was only a fragment of splintered rock.

Meanwhile, the guns and the aeroplanes had been doing their work. The gates and walls were in ruins ; the town was ablaze in a dozen places ; a great pall of smoke was rising heavenwards. And still that pitiless rain of high explosive was poured upon the city. The place was an inferno. It seemed impossible that there could be any living thing remaining within those ruined walls.

We were within a hundred yards of the main gates when suddenly the barrage lifted, revealing the smoking desolation beyond.

"Charge !" came the order.

We swept forward in a thunder of hoofs. The Druses poured a murderous rifle-fire into our ranks, but nothing could stop us. They met us in the gateway and streets, men and women fighting shoulder-to-shoulder with sword and knife. The women swung the two-handed swords with the fury of Amazons.

We cut them down, shot them, and rode over them, driving the survivors before us.

It was all over within an hour. All that remained was for the ruins to be searched in case any Druses might still be lurking among them, and then all would be in readiness for the general to make his triumphal entry.

France had won another great victory.

And my luck had held again.

The wounded were carried off to an improvised

hospital ; the dead were buried ; barricades were set up in case the enemy should attempt a counter-attack.

Having borne the brunt of the attack and having suffered heavier losses than all the rest of the troops combined—that being the Legion's sole purpose—we had a comparatively easy time.

Our chief occupation was looting.

CHAPTER XII

A MONG the men who had joined us at Damascus was an American named Clare, and a friendship had soon sprung up between us. I was fed-up with foreigners and he was the next best thing to an Englishman.

He had joined the Legion for the sake of the adventure and was completely disillusioned by the time that he reached Damascus. He objected to being treated as human refuse; and he objected equally strongly to being used as cannon fodder. Like me, he had come to the conclusion that he had not received a square deal. His motive for joining had been adventure, not an alternative to suicide.

"Say, bo," he remarked to me a few days after the capture of Scueida, "I'm just fed to the back teeth with this God-darned outfit. What about beating it?"

It was an attractive suggestion. Moreover, we

were within fifty or sixty miles of Palestine, which, of course, was under British protection. We might never get such a favourable opportunity again.

We had been talking the idea over and working out a plan when the news reached me that Hans was missing.

Hans was a big fat German attached to the transport section. His chief complaint against the Legion was that there was no beer and he was always talking about his far-off Fatherland. When he was drunk tears used to stream down his fat cheeks as he sang with tremendous fervour sentimental effusions about Gretchen or some other *madchen*. His great pal was Serdik, a Hungarian, who was also in the transport section.

It was a fight in the streets of Scueida that led to the discovery that Hans was in love. After the battle the chiefs of the villages for miles around came hurrying into the town to impress upon the general how devoted was their loyalty to France. The captain had warned us that, the general being in the town, these visitors were not to be robbed or otherwise interfered with. He pointed out that brass hats had peculiar views on how "friendly" natives should be treated.

One morning after another batch of village

chiefs had arrived, the captain noticed a free
fight in progress near our transport lines and
sent me to investigate. I found Hans and
the faithful Serdik struggling with a number of
Arabs.

The Arabs must have mistaken me for somebody
of importance, for they left Hans and told me a
long story about how one of their women had been
insulted by the fat dog of an infidel. I assured
them that the dog would be severely punished,
and with this they went off satisfied.

"You great bladder of lard!" I said to Hans.
"I thought you had more sense than to start
playing the fool with native women!"

"Native women!" he screamed indignantly.
"She is nothing of the sort!"

It then appeared that Hans had lighted upon
a desert romance. The girl in the case was
wondrously fair, which was explained by the fact
that whilst her father was an Arab chief her
mother had been a Belgian. The latter had died
some years ago and the chief was now making
arrangements to give his daughter in marriage
with one of his friends.

Noticing the girl, Hans had introduced himself
and ascertained these details. The *tête-à-tête*,
however, had been interrupted by the chief, who

did not, apparently, hold the same high opinion of legionnaires as his daughter.

Hans maintained that the girl was everything that was delightful, and that it was his divinely-appointed task to save her from being forced to marry a man old enough to be her grandfather.

Hans, fifteen stone of Teuton stolidity, was obviously not designed by Nature for this knight-errant business, and I told him not to be a fool. Serdik expressed the opinion that no girl was worth the risk of an Arab knife between one's shoulders. Hans's answer was to offer to fight the two of us.

A few days later Serdik came to me early one morning with the news that Hans had gone off shortly before dawn. He prophesied gloomily that his friend would be murdered by the Arab chief or, failing that, would be captured and shot as a deserter. The girl would inevitably prove false. In any case, it was a physical impossibility for Hans to tramp the sixty miles of sun-baked wilderness which lay between him and the frontier, especially as he had taken neither food nor water with him. In these circumstances, the faithful Serdik appealed to me to do what I could to bring back his erring friend.

As the captain's batman I had nothing in

particular to do, so I went along and obtained permission to take my horse out for a gallop beyond the town. For a couple of hours I searched among the hills and rocks. But there was no sign of the missing Hans, and at length I returned to the town.

Some time later the Arab chief arrived with the news that his daughter and two of his fleetest horses were missing. There was the usual fuss and bother, but nothing could be done. Hans and his bride were safely across the frontier.

Poor Serdik was very disconsolate. He prophesied that Hans would find matrimony even worse than life in the Legion. He would soon be sighing for the company of his old friend and the mules of the transport section.

The success of Hans encouraged Clare and myself to push forward with our plans. There were no lovelorn maidens, Arab or half-caste, to help us by stealing horses, but we were not worrying about that. We preferred to carry through the business without any romantic entanglements.

Finding that two Germans, Lass and Weiner, were also planning to escape, we took them into our confidence and arranged to make it a joint effort.

Our plans were simple. The first step was to

accumulate such supplies as we could without exciting suspicion. We would then start as soon as possible after nightfall and make for the frontier, setting our direction by the stars. We would travel by night and rest during the day. It was also decided to take a rifle and ammunition, in case of emergencies.

We wasted as little time as possible, for at any moment we might receive orders which would take us away from Scueida, perhaps to some distant desert post.

We did not mention a word about our plans and kept apart as much as possible in order to avoid giving rise to any suspicion.

There were times, perhaps, during that period of preparation when I felt a little doubtful. I would have been happier if Georgia had been coming with us. But I knew that it would be useless to invite him to join in the enterprise. Escape offered him nothing and the Legion was all that he had left in this world.

And then there was the captain. I did not want to leave him. Somehow it was difficult to imagine a life from which he was absent. During the past few months everything had circled around him.

But these doubts were merely momentary. I wanted to escape from all this horror. I wanted to be free and no longer a galley slave ; I wanted to be a man again and master of my fate. Why should I be classed as human refuse, the scum of Europe ?

At last all was in readiness for the great adventure. Darkness fell and each of us made his way to the appointed meeting-place.

As we climbed over a ruined wall and made for the desert beyond I could hardly realize that the great adventure was happening at last. It was all so sudden and so unexpected in spite of the fact that for months my determination to escape had been growing steadily stronger. I could not visualize the fact that on the morrow I should be missing from the squadron, that I had seen the last of the captain, Georgia, Sergeant Crukov, and all the others. It seemed impossible.

We had six water-bottles, six large tins of bully beef, some biscuits, a rifle and two hundred and fifty rounds of ammunition. Clare led the way ; the two Germans followed ; and I brought up the rear with the rifle.

Like shadows we slipped silently through the darkness, expecting every instant to be challenged and fired at by some sentry on the walls. Nobody saw us, however, and after a few minutes we began to breathe more freely.

We walked in silence, Clare setting our course by the stars. Every few minutes I glanced back over my shoulder, wondering whether we were being pursued. But there was little fear of that; it would be morning before it would be discovered that we were missing. It would be then that we should have to face the danger of pursuit. Perhaps they would send out a mounted patrol to search for us. They would have no difficulty in guessing the direction in which we had gone.

A queer shudder swept through me at the thought that soon I might find myself engaged in a life and death struggle with my own comrades.

Hours passed and still we plodded on at a steady, swinging pace, our one idea being to put as many miles as possible between us and Scueida before daylight. Nobody had said a word since we had started—our thoughts were too full and our nerves too tense for chattering. Around us the hyenas and the jackals were busy with their nightly chorus.

Suddenly Clare stopped short.

"Lie down!" he whispered. "Don't make the slightest sound!"

We flung ourselves down.

A neigh came out of the darkness. It was

followed by the soft thudding of hoofs and the clink of steel. Twenty or thirty Druse horsemen cantered past us like white-robed ghosts, so close that we could almost touch them.

Pressed flat against the sand, the sweat standing in beads on my forehead, and my heart beating like thunder in my ears, I lay gripping my rifle. At any rate, I would finish off a few more of the enemies of France before I handed in my ticket.

But they failed to notice us and clattered away into the darkness. Without a word we rose to our feet and continued our march.

Our nerves were on edge and I found myself quivering as if with the ague. We were haunted by the fear of pursuit, tortured by the fear of what might be lying ahead. Our ears strained to catch the slightest sound ; our eyes peered into the darkness. On and on we plodded, every step taking us nearer the Union Jack and freedom.

At length the dawn broke and found us deadbeat. We had marched the whole night through and one mile across the desert is equal to three under ordinary conditions.

Fortunately there was a heap of rocks near at hand and among them we found a cave. Flinging ourselves down, we ate a few scraps of bully and biscuits, moistened our mouths, and then slept the sleep of utter exhaustion.

I was awakened by Clare shaking my shoulder.

"We're done for !" he said.

I jumped up and grabbed my rifle. "What's up ?" I gasped. "The French ?"

"No," he replied. "Those—Boches have drunk all the water !"

Four out of the six water-bottles were dry and another was half-empty. And there were at least thirty miles of desert between us and a fresh supply.

Outside the cave, Lass and Weiner were complacently snoozing in the shade of a rock.

"What the hell have you been doing, you dirty swine ?" I demanded, rousing them with a couple of kicks.

"*Schwein !* Vat you mean, *hein* ?"

"You've drunk all the water, blast you !"

"Vell, ve vas thirsty ! Plenty more water, *hein* ?"

"Plenty more be——! God knows where or when we'll find the next drop ! Anyhow, you two perishing Boches won't get a drop of what's left !"

It was useless to argue about it. The damage had been done. Besides, the sun was so fierce that it was impossible to do anything more than curse.

We spent the rest of the day in snarling silence—staring out across the shimmering desert—wondering if we were being pursued—wondering how many miles still remained between us and the frontier.

The action of those two fools in guzzling the water had more than jeopardized our chances of success. We might strike a village with a pond or a well before we reached the frontier, but that would mean betraying our presence to the Arabs. And we knew that they were not to be trusted.

Could we reach the frontier on the small supply that we had left ? It was more than doubtful. It was impossible to march quickly over the sand, and we had reckoned that it would take us at least three nights to complete the journey.

If only we had a map ! If only we knew our exact position and how many miles there remained before us ! But we could be certain of nothing. All we knew was that we were somewhere between Scueida and the frontier, and that we had one and a half bottles of water.

There was only one thing to be done—push on and hope for the best. There could be no turning back. We had made our throw against Fate and must abide by it.

Perhaps we had made more progress than we dared hope. Perhaps in a few hours we should be safe in a British post and laughing at our fears.

Perhaps!

I was determined to win through. For months I had been dreaming of all the wonderful things that were going to happen—when I had escaped. I was going to make a fresh start. Nothing was impossible.

I would not be cheated of my dreams at the last moment.

Once or twice the two Germans glanced longingly towards the water-bottles, but we refused to allow them to touch them.

"You'd better be careful," I told them. "If Clare and I were anything but a couple of fools we'd leave you here to die and carry on by ourselves. There's just about enough water there to take two of us to the frontier."

They kept quiet after that, and became almost cringing in their friendliness.

Perhaps we were a couple of fools not to leave them to their fate, but—well, even life in the Legion had not dragged us down to that level.

There was a price too heavy to pay, even for life and freedom.

Late in the afternoon we had a meal and drank a few more drops of our precious water, and at sunset started off again on the trail for freedom.

For hour after hour we plodded on in silence. The stars were gleaming like fireflies in the velvet shroud of the night. The jackals and hyenas were howling their hideous psalms to the moon.

Each hour seemed an eternity. My legs were aching with weariness and the sand seemed to be clinging to my feet. The rifle was becoming heavier every moment ; my head was buzzing. I was beginning to suffer the agonies of thirst.

The Germans began to protest that they could go no further. They must rest, just for a little while. They whined and prayed for a drink.

We shared out the last of the beef and the last of the water. Then we continued on our way. Our only chance was to cross the frontier before dawn. We had no means of knowing how far it was distant. We only knew that it seemed as if we had been tramping for hundreds of miles across the desert. It might be that the frontier was nearer than we dared hope. It might be that during the darkness we would stagger across the line which meant the difference between death and freedom.

On and on we stumbled, forcing ourselves forward. The two Germans became light-headed and began to babble and sing in croaking voices. Clare and I cursed them, but for the most part we carried on in silence.

Sounds carry far in the desert and there was no saying who might hear the babbling of the two Germans. At any moment Arabs, Druses, or even French might come to investigate. But Clare and I were past worrying about what might happen. And, in any case, it was impossible to stop them.

My tongue was swollen ; my feet felt raw. The weight of the rifle and the ammunition was dragging on my shoulders like some monstrous burden. The air seemed hot and salt, and every breath I took added to my torturing thirst.

On and on through the interminable night we tramped.

It was worth it, I kept telling myself. Soon we would be across the frontier and laughing at our troubles.

I had been in a worse corner than this at Rashaya, and my luck had held. My luck would pull me through again.

Even in that desperate position I could not visualize the possibility of failure. Somehow we would manage to scrape through.

I wondered what Georgia was doing—I would write to him as soon as I had the chance. I pictured the captain, cursing and swearing when he found that we had made off. I wondered whom he would choose as his batman in my place.

I began to wonder what would happen when at last we reached a British post. It would be great to hear English voices and taste English food again. I could see myself holding a cup of steaming tea. Tea ! I had forgotten there was such a thing ! It was like the elixir of life !

We should be taken to Jerusalem, I supposed. The various consuls would look after us. Lass and Weiner would be sent back to Germany.

Clare and I were going to make for South America. There were fortunes to be made there.

Perhaps I would meet Houssmann and Louise.

On and on I tramped behind the shadowy, staggering forms before me.

It seemed an eternity since we had started.

I took to counting my paces—one—two—three —and told myself that each one was taking me nearer to freedom.

Once I thought I heard the beat of hoofs

behind me. Our pursuers at last! Fumbling at my rifle I swung round with a crazy snarl, ready to fight the whole French Army.

But it was only my imagination. I turned and stumbled on after the others.

At last the dawn came. Still we tramped on, our aching eyes searching the widening horizon.

Had we crossed the frontier? Was there water near at hand? Or had we passed wells and ponds during the night?

We must find water! We could not face the furnace of the day without the means of moistening our mouths. We must find water!

"There's something!" croaked Clare at last, pointing towards the left.

We pushed on eagerly, confident that we were going to find water.

It was a ruined village that we had discovered. Apparently it had been bombed by the French a considerable time before. We staggered about the silent ruins, but there was no sign of water. Anything in the nature of a well had been destroyed.

We flung ourselves down in the shade of what was left of a wall and lay like logs.

The sun was already beating down with a pitiless ferocity. The heat-waves were shimmering above the sand and the stones. High overhead a vulture was hovering in the limitless blue.

For some time we just lay where we had dropped, too exhausted to move, too sick at heart to think. I was conscious only of my thirst. My whole being was aching for water. My tongue was swollen ; my brain was like a furnace.

At length I forced myself to stir.

"What's to be done ?" I asked, turning to Clare.

He sat up and gazed at me with his wild, bloodshot eyes. The two Germans were lying as if they were dead.

"Guess there's only one thing we can do," replied Clare at length. "Carry on till we drop. It's our only chance—such as it is."

I nodded.

It was useless to remain there in the blistering heat without food or drink. We should be dead before nightfall. We might as well blunder blindly on across the wilderness until at last we dropped from sheer exhaustion. Perhaps one of us would hold out longer than the others. Perhaps one would stagger through to life and freedom.

It was our only chance.

We managed to get the semi-conscious Germans on to their feet again and started off afresh, swaying and stumbling under the blazing sun. I had my eyes closed, unable to bear the glare.

God knows how long that desperate march continued or how many miles we covered. I had lost all sense of time.

I could feel myself slipping towards unconsciousness. I saw flashes of Piccadilly, Cardiff crowds on a Saturday night, the drear slag heaps of Abertysswg, coal tips stark against a Welsh sky. It was the beginning of the end.

I was still walking mechanically, but sooner or later I would topple forward on my face.

I wondered whether that vulture was still circling in the sky overhead.

This was the end. My luck had given out at last. The jackals would get me, after all.

Suddenly Clare gripped me by the arm.

"Look! Look!" he croaked.

I opened my aching eyes and saw a native village dancing before me in the sunlight. And midway between us and the village was an Arab carrying two great water-skins slung across his shoulders.

For some moments I stared at him in a dazed sort of way, unable to believe my eyes. Then, gripping my rifle, I staggered towards him. I shouted to him—in a broken whisper.

At last he saw me and stopped.

"Water !" I gasped, pointing to his water-skins.

"How much you give ?" he asked with a sly smile.

I emptied my pockets of all the wealth I possessed—about twenty francs. His eyes gleamed as I poured it into his hands.

I took a long drink from the water-skin, bathed my head and wrists, and filled the empty water bottles. I could feel reason and strength returning to me, the blood tingling and dancing in my veins. I was alive again !

Slinging the water-skins across his shoulder, the Arab continued on his way towards the village. Laughing and singing crazily, I hurried back to rejoin the others.

Clare and Lass snatched the water-bottles from me and gulped down their precious contents. But Weiner had reached breaking-point and was lying unconscious on the sand.

We did our best to bring him round, moistening his lips, bathing his temples and chafing his hands. After a time he opened his eyes and was able to sit up and take a drink.

"Help him across to those rocks," said Clare to Lass. "He'll be better in the shade."

The two were staggering away towards the shelter of the rocks when a dozen Arabs approached us from the village, the chief at their head.

Clare and I stood waiting for them.

"Peace be with you," said the chief, halting within a few yards of us.

"The same be with you," I answered, holding my rifle ready. "But stay where you are."

He asked where we were going, but I answered that that was no business of his.

"I know you," he said. "You belong to the bloodthirsty Legion. You desert."

"Maybe," I agreed. "But if you'll show us the way to the British frontier I'll give you this rifle and all the ammunition I have."

He gazed at me with narrowing eyes for some moments; then began to fumble in his burnouse.

"Is your hand sick?" I asked.

"No."

"Then take it out—quick!"

I emphasized this last remark by bringing my rifle to my shoulder. He started back—and a Mauser pistol fell from his burnouse.

I shot him. It was a case of his life or ours.

The others bolted for the village. Clare and I

made for the pile of rocks where Lass and Weiner were waiting for us.

We found them in a state of great excitement.

"Look!" cried Lass, from the top of a great boulder.

We clambered up beside them and saw, not five hundred yards away, a small stone-built fort with the French flag flying above it!

The temperature was a hundred and something, but I could feel the marrow freezing in my spine as I gazed at that fort and flag.

A few minutes before we had been within an ace of dying of thirst. Chance had saved us— only to fling us face to face with this fresh crisis. It would need a miracle to save us.

I realized now why that Arab chief had refused my offer of the rifle and ammunition. Living under the very noses of the French, he had not dared. It would pay him better to prove his loyalty by capturing us and handing us over.

Spat!

A bullet struck the boulder not half a dozen inches from my leg. Several more followed.

About fifty Arabs were advancing upon us from the village, determined to avenge their chief and prove their loyalty to France.

259

We scrambled down and took cover behind the rocks. It would have been wiser probably to surrender. But I was not in a condition for clear thinking. My first instinct on being attacked was to defend myself.

Gripping my rifle, I brought down the foremost Arab. I got three more with the next few shots. Then, as I was pressing a fresh clip into the magazine, they were upon us, climbing up the rocks like cats.

I brought down one with the butt of my rifle, but another sprang forward and wrenched it from me. After the privations and anxieties of our journey from Scueida our position was hopeless. We were as weak as kittens and outnumbered by ten to one.

And, to clinch matters, a French patrol from the fort arrived on the scene to see what all the bother was about.

A few minutes later we were being half-carried, half-led to the fort. Fortunately the corporal in charge of the post was a good-hearted fellow. He gave us rum and hot food and then left us to sleep as long as we liked.

It was the following morning when we awakened, and never have coffee and rye bread tasted better than they did on that occasion.

The genial corporal came in and chatted with us.

"How far do you think you are from the British frontier?" he asked when we had told him our story.

"Anything between ten and fifteen miles, I suppose."

"Come with me," said the corporal.

Followed by our guards, we accompanied him to the top of the observation tower.

"*Voilà !*" exclaimed the corporal with a dramatic gesture.

Not a mile away was a little cluster of huts with the Union Jack flying above them.

We had been captured on the frontier itself! If only we had stumbled on a few more hundred yards we would have reached the Promised Land!

After all that we had endured—after those terror-ridden nights and sun-scorched days—after exhaustion, hunger, thirst, madness—this was the end! We had failed when success was within our grasp.

"It is the irony!" remarked the corporal.

I said nothing. I just stood and gazed at that fluttering flag, at the figures moving about among the huts.

My heart was dead.

I could not think ; I could not realize what had happened. In a numb, blank sort of way I stood gaping at the freedom I had come so near to winning and had lost.

"*Allons !*" said the corporal.

In silence we stumbled down the stairs of the observation tower—back to the cells.

CHAPTER XIII

A CAPTIVE

THE corporal in charge of the frontier post at Tisse Taibe was the last person to treat me as a human being for many a long day.

We were taken to some sort of a town where we were thrown into a dungeon and given a loaf of bread and a jug of water. The place was underground and only a few stray beams of light managed to struggle in through the tiny window. Rats scampered about the floor, fighting for our food. After a time a few lice-ridden blankets were thrown in to us.

The day after our arrival, four Syrian guards with their bayonets fixed entered the cell. They were followed by a French officer.

"The first swine that touches me, shoot him like a dog!" he remarked to the guards.

We were lined up against the wall.

"What nationality are you?" he demanded.

"English, sir," I replied.

"Ah, English bandits! Insolent swine always!"
And before I could realize what was happening, he
had knocked me down. Fortunately, I was too
weak and depressed to defend myself. If I had I
should doubtless have been shot.

He kicked me as I lay, and then passed on to
the others.

"You will be shot to-morrow," was his parting
remark.

We spent ten days and nights with the rats in
that dark dungeon and then were taken to
Damascus.

Chained two and two, alive with lice, coatless,
our shirts in tatters, filthy and unshaven, we were
marched from the station to the citadel amidst
the jeers of the populace.

On our arrival we were paraded before the
adjutant, who informed us that we were to be
court martialled for deserting in face of the enemy
and for murdering Christian Arabs. He warned
us that the penalty, if we were found guilty—
and he had little doubt on that point—would be
death.

I protested that we had not deserted in face of
the enemy, our departure having been several
days after the defeat of the Druses at Scueida,

and that our crime was that of abandoning our post while in reserve. This may seem a minor point to the layman, but it was of tremendous importance to us. It represented the difference between murder and manslaughter. The penalty for desertion in face of the enemy was death; the usual punishment for abandoning post in reserve was a year's imprisonment. Never have I been more eloquent than I was on that occasion.

As for murdering the Arabs, I maintained that this was in self-defence. I also reminded him that I had murdered dozens of Arabs in the service of France in the course of our tax-gathering expedition on the way to Rashaya. Finally, I asked to be allowed to see the British consul.

This was granted, and never was a man more welcome than the consul. He gave me clean clothes, food, chocolate, magazines, cigarettes, money, and promised to do everything in his power to get the charge reduced to that of abandoning post in reserve.

About a week later the court martial was held. Under an armed guard we were marched into a large room where the bench of officers were awaiting us. The president was a hard-looking, grey-haired colonel. A young lieutenant had been detailed to manage our defence, but I don't think he said more than half a dozen words throughout the proceedings.

Nothing was said about murdering the Arabs, and that charge evidently had been dropped. As to the desertion, it was apparently left to the court to decide whether it was in face of the enemy or whilst in reserve.

"Why did you desert ?" I was asked.

I told them that I had been persuaded to join the Legion by false promises. I considered that I had been swindled.

"You know the penalty for desertion ?"

"Yes, sir. For abandoning post whilst in reserve, one year's imprisonment."

"But you deserted in face of the enemy."

"No, sir. There were no enemy. They had been completely defeated at Scueida a few days before and the survivors were in flight across the desert."

This was a good point and it had an obvious effect upon my judges. Each of them squared his shoulders and gave his moustache a twirl, as if to infer that he had played a great part in the glorious victory at Scueida.

"But you instigated the others to desert," suggested one of the court.

"No, sir. We planned it together."

The young lieutenant who was supposed to be conducting our defence, did not ask me a single question. The prosecutor naturally was not concerned with any of the points in my favour, and he did not give me a chance to bring any of them forward. But my alleged counsel might at least have asked me a few questions about my career in the Legion, so that consideration could have been given to the fact that at Mesmie and Rashaya, as well as at Scueida, I had done my full share of the task of slaughtering the enemies of France. He maintained, however, a pained and dignified silence. Perhaps he was afraid of injuring his own career. Perhaps he was a friend of the prosecutor. In any case, he was worse than useless.

If only we had had our captain to speak for us! He would not have been afraid to tell the truth! Probably he would have ventilated some of his own grievances about the scandalous way in which the Legion was consistently starved of supplies and ammunition. He would have said something, and said it forcefully.

After the prosecutor had asked us his questions, we were marched out whilst the court considered the verdict.

Whether our defending counsel made an eloquent speech on our behalf in our absence, I don't know. But he must have been very brief, for within a few minutes we were marched back into the court.

Clare and I were sentenced to eight years imprisonment each, and the two Germans to five years each.

"Have you anything to say ?" we were asked.

"Yes, a hell of a lot !" answered Clare. He was proceeding to tell them what he thought of them when the guards interrupted his eloquence and bundled him out of the room.

The Germans said nothing. I protested against the sentence as excessive and asked whether any consideration had been given to my record since I had joined the Legion, and whether my captain had been asked to submit a report on my conduct at the battles of Mesmie, Rashaya, and Scueida.

The court dismissed my protest with a shrug of the shoulders and I was marched away to the dungeons of Damascus citadel.

There could be no appeal, no hope of mercy. The prosecutor, evidently, had taken the view that if I had not deserted in face of the enemy and so incurred the death penalty, I had come very near to it and deserved a severe sentence. The judges had agreed with him.

I flung myself down on the stone floor of the cell and lay staring blankly into space.

There were eight years of living death before me.

CHAPTER XIV

PRISON

ARAB mothers tell their children that devils live in Damascus citadel. I believe them.

For centuries untold tortures and hideous horrors have been going on behind those grim walls, endowing those ancient stones with a malign personality. None can escape that fetid spirit. To glance at the place is to shudder ; to live within it is hell. The devils of the citadel transform men into ghouls, lusting for blood and human agony.

I had read and heard of the Inquisition, of the rack, the thumbscrew and the "boot". I had congratulated myself on living in an enlightened age when such things were impossible. In Damascus citadel I had the evidence of my own eyes to prove that these horrors exist to-day.

We were browbeaten and bullied. The slightest offence, real or imagined, meant a slash with a whip. Our food consisted of the coarsest bread,

271

watery soup, and stinking horse-flesh. What was left was given to the Syrian prisoners, who were treated even worse than we were. I have seen those wretched creatures fighting for the putrid scraps of meat which even our hungry stomachs had rebelled against.

We had our meals in mess-rooms, where we were duly visited by the orderly officer accompanied by a sergeant. The latter carried a whip —by way of encouraging complaints. One day the officer happened to take his stand within a few feet of a dixie containing the horsemeat which was about to be served out to us. After a few moments he caught the full savour.

"*Mon Dieu!*" he exclaimed, holding his nose. "Has someone died?"

"It's only the meat, sir," explained the sergeant. "Any complaints?" he added in a roar, gripping his whip.

Of course, nobody dared complain, and the orderly officer was able to report that everything was perfectly satisfactory.

The white prisoners were employed on various fatigues, and this, in addition to breaking the monotony of existence in damp, rat-ridden dungeons, enabled us to see what went on in the citadel.

Executions took place at the rate of about ten a week. In addition to these, there were the prisoners who died "by accident" and those who mysteriously disappeared. We never learnt the truth concerning those disappearances, but there were hints that the river could still tell some ghastly stories.

It was a daily occurrence for a party of Syrians to be brought in, the charge against them usually being that of firing on the French. They were flogged, starved, and sometimes tortured to death. They never received the formality of a trial—in most cases, I imagine, because the evidence against them was of the flimsiest character.

On one occasion I assisted at the "reception" of five old Arabs, the youngest of whom could not have been less than sixty, who were alleged to have taken part in an attack on a train.

These old men, whose guilt had yet to be proved, were hustled into a cell, stripped naked and their wrists tied. They were then flung on the floor and flogged by a huge Senegalese until skin and flesh were cut off their backs. The officer in charge smoked a cigarette as he watched.

The victims screamed and sobbed, their backs raw masses of blood and torn flesh, until at length they collapsed on the stone floor and only an occasional feeble moan told that they still lived.

With the blood dripping from his whip the Senegalese stepped back and grinned, his eyes gleaming in his black face, and his teeth showing.

I was faint with horror. I longed to feel my fingers choking the life out of that black throat. The brute could flog defenceless old men and smile; but I had seen how he and his like behave when there was real fighting to be done. I remembered those gibbering, panic-stricken wretches at Rashaya and Scueida.

But I could do nothing. I was a prisoner, a mere cipher existing only to obey the orders of my superiors.

"The salt," said the officer, turning to us.

We took two large buckets of brine and, standing over the half-dead victims, flung the salt water over their tortured bodies and into their bleeding wounds.

The bodies writhed and doubled in agony. Hideous screams filled the air. One man sprang a full yard into the air and then dropped senseless.

We dragged them into a dark cell where they were left with the rats to recover or die as chance might decide.

These unfortunate wretches were merely

suspected of the offence with which they were charged, probably on the word of some spy. But a worse fate awaited those of whose guilt there was no doubt.

By the mercy of Providence I was not a witness of what happened to the Syrian bandit who had murdered two French sergeants. But I could hear.

The ancient torture-chamber, which was known as "the Devil's Cell", was not far from my own dungeon, and I had seen the thumbscrews, the rack, and the other mediæval instruments of torture it contained. I had often shuddered at the thought of those who had met frightful deaths within its centuries-old walls. The place seemed to reek with horror.

In the dead of night I heard the bandit being dragged past my dungeon to "the Devil's Cell". The door clanged and then there was silence.

Suddenly there was a sharp crack, followed by a piercing scream. Then low, fierce voices—muffled sounds—the most terrible cries that ever I have heard—

They shuddered and sobbed through the silence of the night—the agony of a soul in hell. Quivering and gasping, I lay listening. The sweat was pouring down my cheeks.

The screams died down at length, and only a sobbing moan stole through the dark corridors of the citadel of terror.

Then again a high, nerve-shattering scream. A cry to God in Heaven. A crack—was it whip or bone ? A screech.

Then the hushed stillness of the night.

An hour later, it was my duty to take coffee round to the guards. As I passed "the Devil's Cell", I glanced in through the iron grille in the door. In the dim light from the lamp in the corridor I saw a still, huddled form lying in a dark pool of blood.

On my return, I saw two men dragging a sack away from "the Devil's Cell". They passed me with their ghastly burden and entered a neighbouring cell. A few moments later I heard the faint sound of a distant splash.

The river had received another addition to its secrets of a thousand years.

For nights afterwards the echoes of those agonized screams filled the dark corridors of the citadel.

After about a month I left Damascus with a number of other prisoners. Handcuffed two and two, filthy, ragged, and unkempt, we were marched to the railway station where we entrained for

Beyrout. Here we were manacled and herded into the hold of a cargo steamer. The voyage to Marseilles was a nightmare. Chained together, we were herded like galley slaves. We were not allowed to leave the hold and hardly a breath of fresh air reached us. The heat—it was August— was stifling. The empty monotony of the days and nights increased the horror a hundredfold.

At Marseilles we were taken to the Fort St. Nicholas, where we were inspected by the strangest officer I have ever seen. He was a sallow-faced little Corsican, with extraordinarily bright eyes and a tremendous moustache. In his belt he carried two big Mauser pistols.

He rushed up and down the line of human derelicts, occasionally pausing to peer into the face of a man and cry, in a high-pitched voice: "Ha! Bandit! You will burn!"

Whether he was insane or merely being funny, we had no means of ascertaining.

From Marseilles we were taken to Lyons, and thence to Albertville, in Haute Savoi. Here our tattered and verminous rags were taken from us and we were supplied with convicts' clothes. These, at least, were clean, and a Savile Row outfit could not have felt more luxurious.

Albertville was the best of the prisons I sampled

in the course of my wanderings as a convict. Both the treatment and the food were good and the cleanliness was exemplary. Unfortunately, my stay here was short, and after a few days we were moved to Clairvaux, the prison at which I was to serve out my sentence.

We now came under civilian discipline, with the result that we lost our meagre ration of cigarettes —one of the few privileges enjoyed by military prisoners. Several Frenchmen began a hunger strike by way of protest, with the result that they were sent to the dungeons for "correction", which was the official term for flogging. I took no part in the affair, so I was "let off" with a period of solitary confinement by way of a warning. It nearly drove me mad.

The cells at Clairvaux were iron cages about fifteen feet by ten, damp, dark, unheated and unventilated. The sheets were changed once a month and the blankets once every three months —unfortunately, they were filthy when we received them. Our diet consisted of the inevitable "dish-water" soup, coarse bread, rice and potatoes. Once a week we received a portion of horse-flesh.

The sanitation was indescribable, which possibly accounts for the fact that consumption was very prevalent in the prison. To make matters worse, the warders and other officials indulged in all sorts of petty spite at the expense of the prisoners. Anything in the nature of a complaint was always dealt with severely.

There was one man whom consumption had reduced to a living skeleton. The civilian doctor, or his deputy, having pronounced that he was perfectly fit, he asked to be examined by a military doctor. For this act of "insubordination" he was given thirty days in the dungeons.

A week or so later he was carried from the dungeons to the hospital, where he subsequently died of consumption.

On the one occasion on which I went sick, I had an amazing experience. The prisoner who acted as the doctor's clerk was a shrivelled, prematurely aged man, with haunted eyes and a cringing manner. A human rat.

I was telling him my symptoms when suddenly he gasped : "You are English !"

I nodded.

"English !" he muttered, fumbling at his lips and cowering before me in apparent terror.

Thinking that he was going to throw a fit, I called one of the warders who was standing nearby.

"Did you tell him that you were English ?" he asked.

"Yes," I answered, wondering why my nationality should have such an extraordinary effect upon the man.

The warder nodded philosophically. "He's afraid that the English will kill him," he explained. "He says that he's the man who betrayed your Nurse Cavell to the Boches."

I had no means of testing the truth of the statement, but personally I am convinced that cowering wretch was indeed the betrayer of Nurse Cavell. Never have I seen eyes so haunted, a face so eaten with the bitterness of remorse.

Since seeing that prisoner who acted as the doctor's clerk at Clairvaux, I have known what Barrabas looked like.

Religion has never been a speciality of mine, but, looking at that cringing rat, I remembered some words which I had heard in my old Sunday School days.

"It were better for him if a great millstone were hanged about his neck and he were cast into the sea."

I saw no more of him. I don't know what was the crime for which he found himself in Clairvaux,

or what sentence he was serving. Long afterwards I read in a newspaper that the betrayer of
Nurse Cavell was to be tried before a tribunal in
Brussels. Perhaps it was the same man. His
enforced sojourn at Clairvaux would explain the
long delay in bringing him to justice.

Gradually I settled down to the stagnant
existence of a convict. I was no longer alive ; I
was a numbered automaton, without hope or will.

Nothing seemed to matter. Existence had
become an endless succession of empty days and
nights. The world had forgotten me, and I wanted
only to forget.

But, as my friend Georgia had already discovered, to forget is the most difficult of all
achievements. And convicts cannot obtain the
assistance of *vin rouge*.

The nights were the worst. For hours I used
to lie in my dreary cell and wonder what the
captain, Sergeant Crukov, Georgia, and all the
others were doing. Were they still alive, or were
the desert jackals fighting over their bones ?
Perhaps, at that moment, they were beleaguered
in some distant outpost. Of course, the captain
as usual would be cursing at the shortage of
ammunition and expressing his opinion of the
headquarters staff.

I wished I were with them ; sometimes I wished that I had gone under at Scueida. Anything would have been better than this living death.

And I had eight years of this stagnation before me.

Sometimes my memory went rummaging in the past, and I lived again through trivial, long-forgotten incidents—a game of marbles in the school playground, a conversation at the pithead whilst waiting for the cage, sheltering from the rain under a haystack during my tramp to London.

It was curious how unreal the past seemed ; it was composed wholly of dreams. Only Clairvaux was real.

During the day we were employed at various tasks, and for a considerable time I worked as a varnisher.

An Italian who was "in" for five years for robbery was similarly employed, and it was not long before a furtive friendship developed between us.

He had emigrated to South America when a boy and had made a modest fortune. Then, coming to Paris, he had fallen into bad company and lost every penny he possessed. He had also fallen in love with a girl who worked in a café in Montmartre.

It was with a view to marrying the girl and starting afresh in South America that he had robbed a bank clerk.

The girl had not only promised to wait for him to serve his five years' sentence, but had said that she would do her best to arrange for a prison wedding.

Perhaps this touching devotion was partly due to the fact that my friend had hidden the 10,000 francs of which he had robbed the bank clerk and had kept the secret of their hiding-place very strictly to himself. He had every hope that on his release he would find those stolen francs safely waiting for him.

In any case, the girl's persistent and touching appeals must have softened the hearts of the authorities, for one day the permission of the Minister of Justice was received for Convict 1564 to marry Mlle Marie Govert in the prison of Clairvaux.

It was not, however, a very satisfactory wedding. The prison authorities did not provide a feast and invite all the convicts to the jollification. There was no champagne, no flowers, and no wedding march. So far as the rest of us were concerned, everything went on as usual. The bridegroom, too, considered the arrangements open to criticism, for immediately after the ceremony he was parted from his bride and taken back to his varnishing. From his muttered remarks I gathered that he did not appreciate the novelty of the situation and had old-fashioned views on how a wedding should conclude.

I did my best to cheer him up by expressing the belief that on his release he would be sure to find both his bride and his stolen wealth awaiting him. This was certainly a possibility, for even in the excitement of getting married he had taken good care not to tell his bride where he had hidden the money.

I should have liked to meet the lady and discover whether it was true love or the money which provided the motive for her appeal to the Minister of Justice. That, however, is a tantalizing question to which only Convict 1564 could provide the answer. The rest of us, cynics and sentimentalists, can take our choice.

The romance of Convict 1564—a matter of whispered conversations at the varnishing bench, so far as I was concerned—provided all the thrills of a nine-days' wonder, but soon I slipped back into the eternal monotony of my prison existence. The green slime gathered again over the surface of the stagnant pool.

Day followed day and night followed night, each exactly the same as the one before and the one after, each void of hope. I lost all sense of time. Brain and body were numb.

Nothing mattered.

Nobody cared.

I was just a numbered automaton. The only difference between me and the moss on the walls of my prison was the fact that I breathed.

CHAPTER XV

FREEDOM

I HAD served eighteen months of my sentence of eight years.

But I had long since lost interest in months and years. In my living tomb I only knew that an eternity of weariness lay both before and behind me. Nothing could ever happen to break the mechanical routine of my existence.

Then, one morning, my cell door was opened at an hour when it had never opened before. A warder told me to go with him.

In a dazed, bewildered way I followed him. The impossible was happening! The eternal monotony had been broken!

I found myself in what seemed an incredibly luxurious room. The prison governor was seated at a desk.

He spoke about representations having been made by the British Government, about the clemency of France, about my being released and sent back to England.

I could only gape at him in a dazed way. It was impossible. My brain was playing tricks with me. It must be a dream.

Then at last I began to realize the truth.

Something stirred within me. The dawn was breaking.

The Governor finished speaking and turned his attention to some papers lying beside him on the desk. To him it was nothing in particular, just an incident in the day's round.

A warder touched me on the shoulder. The interview was at an end.

My heart was pounding against my ribs as I turned away. I was not forgotten after all. I still had a place in the world. The nightmare was at an end and I was going back to England, back to those dreams of the past.

I was free !

I was John Harvey ! A man once more '

THE END